A Guide to AMERICAN STATES

Utah

THE BEEHIVE STATE

MEDIA ENHANCED BOOKS

AV2 BY WEIGL

ADDED VALUE · AUDIO VISUAL

www.av2books.com

AV² provides enriched content that supplements and complements this book. Weigl's AV² books strive to create inspired learning and engage young minds in a total learning experience.

Your AV² Media Enhanced books come alive with...

Audio
Listen to sections of the book read aloud.

Key Words
Study vocabulary, and complete a matching word activity.

Video
Watch informative video clips.

Quizzes
Test your knowledge.

Go to **www.av2books.com,** and enter this book's unique code.

BOOK CODE

Z944316

Embedded Weblinks
Gain additional information for research.

Slide Show
View images and captions, and prepare a presentation.

AV² by Weigl brings you media enhanced books that support active learning.

Try This!
Complete activities and hands-on experiments.

... and much, much more!

Published by AV² by Weigl
350 5th Avenue, 59th Floor
New York, NY 10118
Website: www.av2books.com   www.weigl.com

Library of Congress Cataloging-in-Publication Data

Parker, Janice.
  Utah / Janice Parker.
    p. cm. -- (A guide to American states)
Includes index.
ISBN 978-1-61690-817-1 (hardcover : alk. paper) -- ISBN 978-1-61690-493-7 (online)
I. Title.
F826.3.P373 2011
979.2--dc23
                          2011019234

Printed in the United States of America in North Mankato, Minnesota

052011
WEP180511

Project Coordinator Jordan McGill
Art Director Terry Paulhus

Photo Credits
Every reasonable effort has been made to trace ownership and to obtain permission to reprint copyright material. The publishers would be pleased to have any errors or omissions brought to their attention so that they may be corrected in subsequent printings.

Weigl acknowledges Getty Images as its primary image supplier for this title.

Contents

More than 2,000 natural sandstone arches are preserved in Arches National Park.

Introduction

U tah is located in the mountain region of the west-central United States. The state's unique terrain includes snowcapped mountains, sparkling lakes, deep valleys, barren salt flats, and remote deserts. Utah also has a rugged plateau region, which features multicolored canyons and impressive rock formations. Utah's varied landscape makes it a great place for recreational activities. The state has five national parks, two national recreation areas, several national monuments, and 45 state parks. Many Utahans enjoy activities such as boating, swimming, fishing, hiking, and skiing. Most of the state receives very little rainfall, which means people can be outdoors enjoying these activities many days of the year.

The Sundance Film Festival is the largest independent film festival in the United States. It has been held annually in Utah since 1978.

The Mount Nebo Wilderness Area covers more than 28,000 acres. Mount Nebo, located in this area, is the highest point in the Wasatch mountain range.

Visitors to Utah will be amazed by the state's wealth of historical spots. At This Is the Place Heritage Park, people can experience a historic village that re-creates life in a typical Utah community of the mid-1800s. This park remembers the many people who have called Utah home over the years. Early residents of the region that became Utah include American Indians, Spanish explorers, Mormon pioneers, and mountain men.

Early Mormon settlers dealt with low rainfall in the region by building **irrigation** systems. Many Mormons worked hard and became very successful at farming the land. They built settlements and grew prosperous. Today the total area of farmland in Utah is relatively small, yet it is productive. Hay, corn, barley, and wheat are the state's main crops, but livestock and livestock products earn Utah farmers the most money.

Where Is Utah?

Utah's location in the west is about halfway between Canada to the north and Mexico to the south. Utah has one international airport, in Salt Lake City. The Salt Lake City International Airport is used by more than 20 million people every year. Visitors to Utah can take advantage of the bus services that connect the state's main cities. Utah also offers road travelers more than 40,000 miles of public highways.

The first commercial passenger flight from Salt Lake City International Airport took off in 1926. Today, nearly 750 flights leave the airport daily.

Utah offers an array of cultural sites and activities, including festivals and theater houses. The state boasts dozens of museums and outdoor attractions that appeal to a wide variety of interests. There are art galleries and national parks. The state also has many science-based attractions, such as botanical gardens and zoos.

In Utah's early years, mining and farming were key economic activities, and this is still the case. In more recent years, though, the state's manufacturing and tourism industries have grown considerably. Utah's national parks, monuments, and ski resorts, along with the annual Sundance Film Festival, have helped the state become a popular destination for tourists. Nearly 5 million people visited Utah's state parks in 2010.

I DIDN'T KNOW THAT!

Utah is divided into 29 counties.

Utah's nickname, The Beehive State, comes from the state's original name. It was called Deseret, a word from *The Book of Mormon* meaning "Land of the Honeybee." The beehive is a symbol of Utahans' hard work and industry.

Salt Lake City was originally named Great Salt Lake City. "Great" was dropped from the name in 1868.

Most of Utah's ski resorts are open from November to mid-May. Skiers and snowboarders come to Utah from all over the world.

Mapping Utah

S everal other states share a border with Utah. Its neighbors are Idaho and Wyoming to the north, Arizona to the south, Colorado and Wyoming to the east, and Nevada to the west. At the southeast corner of Utah is the Four Corners, the only place in the United States where four state boundaries meet at one point. Arizona, Colorado, and New Mexico are the other Four Corners states. Utah ranks 12th among the states in land area.

Sites and Symbols

STATE SEAL
Utah

STATE BIRD
California gull

STATE FLOWER
Sego lily

STATE FLAG
Utah

STATE FRUIT
Cherry

STATE TREE
Blue spruce

Nickname The Beehive State

Motto Industry

Song "Utah, This Is the Place" by Sam and Gary Francis

Entered the Union January 4, 1896, as the 45th state

Capital Salt Lake City

Population (2010 Census) 2,763,885 Ranked 34th state

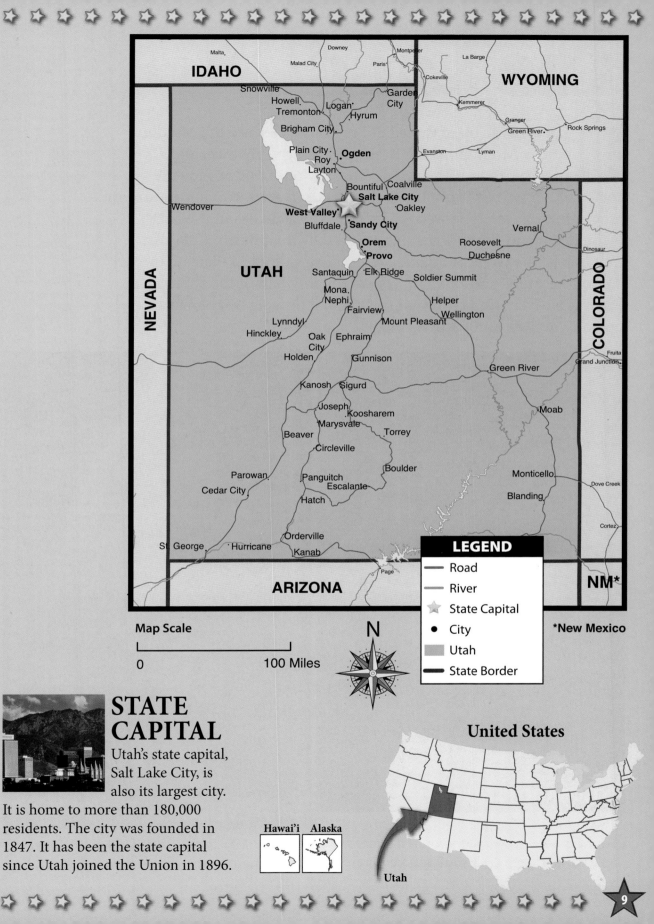

STATE CAPITAL

Utah's state capital, Salt Lake City, is also its largest city. It is home to more than 180,000 residents. The city was founded in 1847. It has been the state capital since Utah joined the Union in 1896.

United States

Hawai'i   Alaska

Utah

LEGEND

— Road
— River
⭐ State Capital
• City
▨ Utah
— State Border

*New Mexico

Map Scale

0   100 Miles

N

The Land

U tah is made up of three land regions. They are the Middle Rocky Mountains, the Basin and Range Province, and the Colorado Plateau. The Rocky Mountains occupy the northeastern part of Utah. Uinta and Wasatch are the major **mountain ranges** in this area. The western third of the state lies in the part of the Basin and Range Province called the Great Basin. This area contains Utah's Great Salt Lake Desert. The Colorado Plateau, in the southeastern part of Utah, covers roughly half of the state. The Colorado River winds through this region, flowing by colorful canyons, arches, and natural bridges.

COLORADO PLATEAU

The Colorado Plateau is centered in the Four Corners region of the United States. Its total land area is 130,000 square miles.

BRIDAL VEIL FALLS

Bridal Veil Falls, a waterfall in Provo Canyon in northern Utah, is more than 600 feet tall.

GREAT SALT LAKE

The Great Salt Lake is the saltiest lake in North America. Very few living creatures can survive in its waters.

MONUMENT VALLEY

Monument Valley is located in the southern part of the state. It is known for its large sandstone formations, which have provided a backdrop to many Western movies.

The Uinta Mountains are the only major range in the United States that runs in an east-west direction.

Erosion from water and temperature changes has created many beautiful and unusual rock formations in the high desert of southeastern Utah.

The state of Utah obtains a large amount of water from the Colorado River and its **tributaries**.

Because winter is mild in most of Utah, people can enjoy outdoor activities year-round.

Climate

U tah's climate differs from region to region. Most of the state enjoys hot, dry summers and mild winters. The average July high temperature in Utah ranges from about 85° Fahrenheit in the mountains to 90° F in the southern part of the state. January high temperatures drop to around 40° F in the south and a chilly 30° F in the mountains. The Great Salt Lake Desert receives less than 5 inches of precipitation per year. The mountain areas, on the other hand, can receive about 40 inches of precipitation each year.

Average January Temperatures Across Utah

The southwestern United States is known for being dry and hot, but parts of Utah can get very cold in the winter. Why might Randolph's winter be so much colder than St. George's?

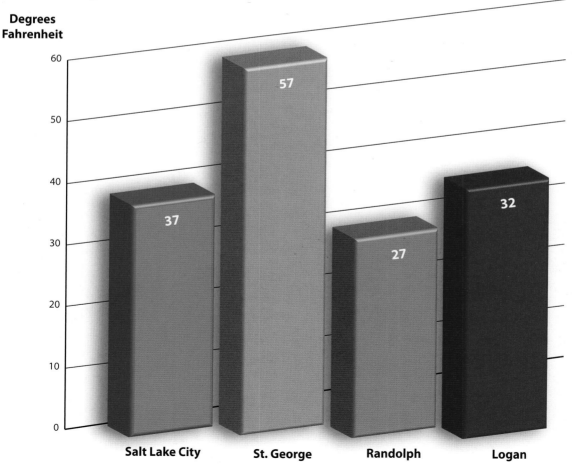

Degrees Fahrenheit

Salt Lake City	St. George	Randolph	Logan
37	57	27	32

Natural Resources

Utah is rich in mineral deposits. The state is a leading producer of copper, most of which is mined in Bingham Canyon. Gold and silver are also mined in Utah. In fact, Utah is one of the nation's leading gold producers. Iron is mined in the southern part of the state. Natural gas, petroleum, and coal are found in the Colorado Plateau. Salt and other minerals are obtained from the Great Salt Lake.

Utah's leading agricultural product is cattle.

Utah's Bingham Canyon Mine is the deepest open-pit mine in the world.

Utah is the only state that produces Gilsonite, which is used in road oil and asphalt tile. Gilsonite has been produced in Utah since the 1880s. Clay, limestone, and gravel are also important to the state.

Soil is another valuable natural resource in Utah. The soil supports many crops, such as hay, wheat, and barley. In addition, much of the land is suitable for grazing livestock.

Copper, which is a good conductor of heat and electricity, was first discovered in Utah in the 1860s.

Dry farming, a farming method that requires very little water, was first practiced in Utah.

More than one quarter of Utah is forested.

Magnesium, cement, potash, and beryllium are all found in Utah.

Plants

There are many forests in Utah. Trees common to the area include firs, pines, aspens, maples, poplars, Utah oaks, and willows, as well as the state tree, the blue spruce. Cacti grow in the desert areas. Wildflowers, including the yucca and the Indian paintbrush, flourish throughout the state.

Flowering plants bloom during the spring and summer in the state's desert regions. At higher elevations in the mountains, strong winds and a short growing season prevent trees from growing to full height. At the highest elevations, only grasses and **annuals** grow.

BEAVERTAIL CACTUS

Many types of cacti grow in Utah, including the beavertail cactus, which gets its name from its resemblance to a beaver's tail.

INDIAN PAINTBRUSH

The colorful Indian paintbrush, which can be yellow, red, orange, or cream colored, grows best in areas with sandy soil.

SEGO LILY

Bulbs of the sego lily were a source of food for Utah's early settlers. This lily was adopted as the state flower in 1911.

SAGEBRUSH

Sagebrush, a common shrub in Utah, has a strong smell that discourages animals from eating it.

The dwarf bearclaw-poppy is an **endangered** plant found only in Washington County.

The prickly pear cactus produces an edible fruit. The fruit can be called a cactus fruit or cactus fig. The fruit's skin, which has spines, must be carefully removed before eating.

The largest member of the yucca family, the Joshua tree, can be found in the Mojave Desert. The tree was named for a Biblical hero by Mormon settlers.

Animals

Many large mammals inhabit Utah. American black bears, mule deer, mountain lions, elk, and pronghorns live in various parts of the state. Porcupines and raccoons are common sights in the forests. Utah's desert animals include wild horses, coyotes, Gila monsters, rattlesnakes, and kangaroo rats. Some desert animals remain in their dens or **burrows** during the middle of the day when temperatures are at their highest. Several animals native to Utah are endangered, including the black-footed ferret and the gray wolf.

Bird-watchers in Utah can spot great horned owls, roadrunners, hummingbirds, and red-tailed hawks in the desert. The state is also home to numerous game birds, including the ring-necked pheasant, the ruffed grouse, and Gambel's quail. There are many eagles and hawks in Utah. Hawkwatch International, an organization created to protect **birds of prey** and their environment, has its headquarters in Salt Lake City.

GAMBEL'S QUAIL

The Gambel's quail, also known as the desert quail or Arizona quail, can be found in the southern part of the state.

UTAH PRAIRIE DOG

The Utah prairie dog is listed as a threatened species. It does not live in any other part of the world.

GILA MONSTER

The only poisonous lizard native to the United States, the Gila monster, can be found in the southwestern corner of Utah.

PORCUPINE

The porcupine can be found in many different habitats but prefers **coniferous** and mixed forest areas.

A fifth-grade class successfully lobbied to make the honeybee the state insect in 1983.

Many birds, such as the Canada goose, the mallard, and the canvasback, pass through Utah as they migrate.

Utah is the site of many dinosaur **fossil** discoveries. Large dinosaur tracks have also been found in the southern part of the state.

Utah's state fish is the Bonneville cutthroat trout.

Tourism

Tourism is a major industry in Utah. People come from all over the world to experience the state's historic sites and natural areas. Summer is the most popular tourist season. Tourists with a taste for daring activities can try river rafting on Utah's rushing waters, as well as rock climbing and mountain biking. In the winter, visitors ski and snowboard at Utah's many ski resorts.

Tourists who visit Arches National Park can ramble around more than 2,000 natural stone arches. Salt Lake City is a popular tourist destination. Temple Square is the most visited site in the city. Brigham Young, an important Mormon leader, selected this location in 1847 for the new settlement's Mormon temple.

DINOSAUR NATIONAL MONUMENT

Visitors to Dinosaur National Monument can watch **paleontologists** digging for dinosaur bones. They can also learn how fossils are cleaned and preserved.

BRYCE CANYON NATIONAL PARK

Bryce Canyon National Park covers more than 37,277 acres in southwestern Utah. The park is famous for the spectacular views created by its brightly colored rocks.

TEMPLE SQUARE

Salt Lake Temple, the largest and best-known Mormon temple in the world, is in Temple Square in Salt Lake City. More than 3 million people visit Temple Square every year.

GRAND STAIRCASE-ESCALANTE NATIONAL MONUMENT

Grand Staircase-Escalante National Monument spans nearly 2 million acres in the southern part of the state.

Salt Lake City hosted the 2002 Winter Olympics, which featured more than 2,300 athletes from 80 nations.

Salt Lake Temple in Salt Lake City took 40 years to build.

More than 18 million tourists travel to Utah each year.

Named for Brigham Young, Brigham City is one of Utah's most popular tourist attractions. It is near the Golden Spike National Historical Site, which marks the 1869 completion of the first **transcontinental** railroad to connect the eastern United States with the Far West.

The city of Kanab is nicknamed "Little Hollywood" because so many Western movies have been filmed there.

Industry

Traditionally, agriculture and mining were important industries in Utah. Today manufacturing, transportation, finance, and other service industries, including tourism, employ many more Utahans than the traditional industries do. Many people in Utah hold seasonal jobs in the tourism industry. In the winter, they may work at ski resorts or hotels that cater to skiers and snowboarders.

Industries in Utah
Value of Goods and Services in Millions of Dollars

Utah has many different kinds of industries. Service industries provide assistance or services to other people. The state's largest employer is a health-care company, which is part of the service industry. What are some services provided by people who work in health care?

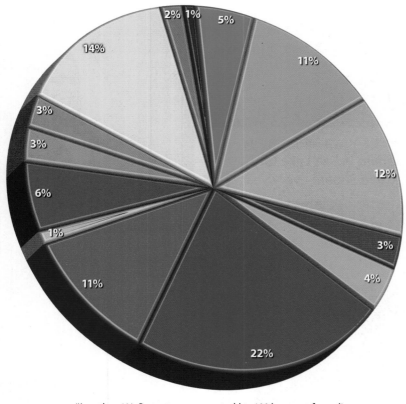

*Less than 1%. Percentages may not add to 100 because of rounding.

LEGEND

* Agriculture, Forestry, and Fishing	$495
Mining	$2,742
Utilities	$1,548
Construction	$6,074
Manufacturing	$12,714
Wholesale and Retail Trade	$13,138
Transportation	$3,862
Media and Entertainment	$4,711
Finance, Insurance, and Real Estate	$25,410
Professional and Technical Services	$12,197
Education	$1,272
Health Care	$6,492
Hotels and Restaurants	$2,956
Other Services	$3,437
Government	$15,893
TOTAL	**$112,941**

Many of Utah's workers are employed in service industries. The many different kinds of service jobs include waiting on tables in restaurants and repairing computers. Other Utahans work in the retail or **wholesale** businesses. Intermountain Health Care, a large chain of hospitals and other health-care facilities, has its headquarters in Salt Lake City. More than 20,000 of Utah's workers were employed by the company as of 2009, making it the state's largest employer.

Robert Redford named the Sundance Film Festival after his part in the 1969 film Butch Cassidy and the Sundance Kid.

The Bonneville Salt Flats, once the bed of an ancient lake, are now the site of high-speed automobile racing.

McDonnell-Douglas, now part of Boeing, began building airplane parts in Utah in 1987.

Brigham Young University employees are generally very happy with their jobs. In a 2010 survey run by CareerBliss.com, BYU employees were ranked the third-happiest among all U.S. higher education institutions.

Goods and Services

Manufacturing Utah has a **diverse** economy. Mining, farming, manufacturing, and tourism are the state's main economic activities. Utah's agricultural industry provides many important goods. Hay is grown to feed livestock. Wheat is grown in the northern parts of the state. Vegetables and fruits, such as potatoes, cherries, peaches, apples, and onions, are grown on irrigated farmland. Greenhouse and nursery products are also produced in Utah.

More than three-quarters of Utah's farm income is obtained from the sale of livestock and livestock products, such as beef, lamb, and dairy products. **Poultry** products, especially turkeys and eggs, are also valuable goods in the state.

More than 15,000 farms can be found in Utah.

Most of Utah's land is not well-suited for growing crops, but it can provide grass for grazing animals.

Many different products are manufactured in Utah, including computers and office equipment. Many types of transportation equipment, ranging from space vehicles to automobile parts, are also manufactured in the state. The chemical industry, which produces medicines, and the food processing industry are very important in Utah. Other products made in the state include medical tools, fabricated metals, and paper goods.

Most of Utah's electricity is generated by steam-driven power plants, which are fueled by low-sulfur coal. Increased coal production in the Colorado Plateau has helped increase the state's mining revenues. Utah also obtains some of its power from hydroelectric plants, which convert to power of moving water into electricity.

I DIDN'T KNOW THAT!

Apple trees were first brought to Utah by some of its early pioneers.

WordPerfect, a popular word-processing program, was created in the late 1970s by Alan Ashton and Bruce Bastian of Brigham Young University. WordPerfect was the business standard in word processing in the 1980s and early 1990s.

Salt Lake City is the state's major business and finance center. Many companies based in Utah have their headquarters in Salt Lake City.

Carbon, Emery, and Sevier counties produce almost all of the state's coal.

Utah is among the top states in producing mink **pelts**.

American Indians

The first people to live in the area that is now Utah were **Paleo-Indians**. It is believed that these people lived in the region from 9,000 to 5,000 BC. These ancient people hunted large animals for food. Later, as the Paleo-Indians learned how to make more advanced hunting weapons, they began to stay in one area rather than follow the animals they hunted. They lived in caves and shelters made from wood and rocks, and they gathered plants and berries for food.

Dwellings built by the Ancestral Puebloan people can be seen in Mule Canyon. The dwellings are more than 700 years old.

About 2,000 years ago, two different groups of American Indians, the Ancestral Puebloan people and the Fremont, lived in the Utah area. The Ancestral Puebloan people lived in southern Utah. They grew corn, squash, and beans and raised turkeys. The Ancestral Puebloan people lived in rock dwellings built into cliffs and canyons. They are known today for the art they carved into, and painted on, the cliffs. The Fremont lived in northern Utah and were hunter-gatherers.

By the 1300s Utah was home to several major groups of American Indians. These groups included the Ute, the Paiute, the Shoshoni, the Goshute, and the Navajo. The largest group was the Ute, who occupied eastern Utah. By the 1800s they lived in tepees and hunted bison, or buffalo.

Today, many Ute live on the Uintah and Ouray Reservation. Covering more than 4.5 million acres, it is the second-largest reservation in the United States.

Explorer Jedediah S. Smith and his men survived several attacks by American Indians during their travels. Smith was eventually killed by Comanche warriors in 1831.

Explorers and Missionaries

I n 1776 a group of explorers led by two Franciscan priests, Francisco Atanasio Domínguez and Silvestre Vélez de Escalante, entered Utah. The Domínguez-Escalante **expedition** was searching for a route from New Mexico to California. The arrival of winter forced the group to return to Santa Fe, New Mexico. Over the next few decades, merchants from Santa Fe traded goods with the American Indians in what is now Utah.

In the early 1800s fur trappers and traders called mountain men explored the region while trapping beavers, minks, and other animals with valuable pelts. In the spring the trappers met for an annual gathering, called a rendezvous. There the trappers bought supplies and traded pelts with American Indians and company agents. They also celebrated the year's success with eating, singing, and contests.

Timeline of Settlement

Early Exploration

1765 Spanish explorer Juan Maria de Rivera is the first European known to have visited Utah.

1776 The Domínguez-Escalante expedition explores the region.

1778 Don Bernardo Miera y Pacheco, a member of the Domínguez-Escalante expedition, draws the first map of Utah.

Further Exploration

1821 After winning independence from Spain, Mexico claims all of what is now Utah.

1824 American Jim Bridger is the first person of European descent to reach the Great Salt Lake.

1827 American Jedediah S. Smith becomes the first person of European descent to cross Utah from north to south and then from west to east.

Travelers and Settlers

1846 The Donner-Reed expedition travels through Utah on its way to California. Dozens of members of the party die later in the journey when they are trapped by harsh winter weather.

1847 Led by Brigham Young, Mormon settlers arrive in Salt Lake Valley.

Statehood

1848 Most of the Southwest, including Utah, is transferred from Mexico to the United States at the end of the Mexican-American War.

1850 The U.S. government establishes the Utah Territory, which originally includes parts of Nevada, Colorado, and Wyoming, as well as present-day Utah.

1896 Utah, with its present boundaries, becomes the 45th state on January 4.

Early Settlers

T he U.S. government sent people to explore and settle the Utah area. In 1843, John Charles Frémont, a government explorer, visited the Great Salt Lake area. He returned to the region in 1845. Frémont mapped trails in Utah and described the plant and animal life he encountered in the Great Basin.

Map of Settlements and Resources in Early Utah

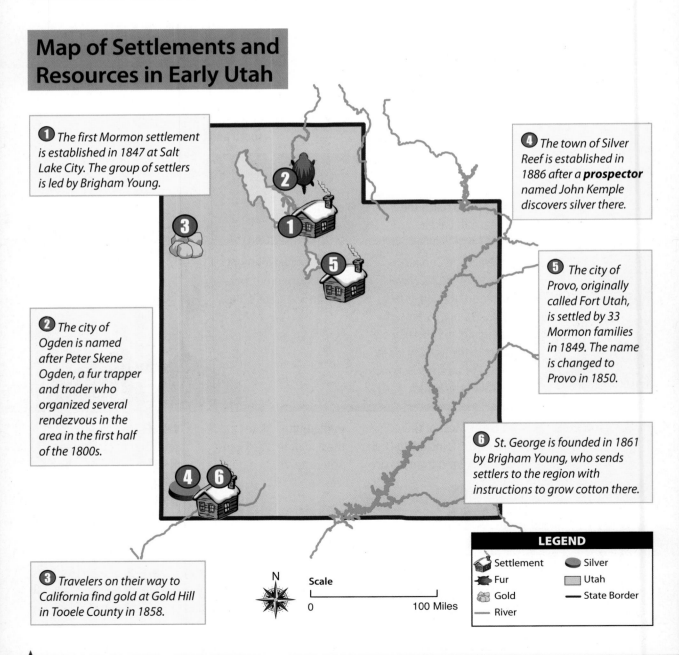

1 The first Mormon settlement is established in 1847 at Salt Lake City. The group of settlers is led by Brigham Young.

4 The town of Silver Reef is established in 1886 after a **prospector** named John Kemple discovers silver there.

2 The city of Ogden is named after Peter Skene Ogden, a fur trapper and trader who organized several rendezvous in the area in the first half of the 1800s.

5 The city of Provo, originally called Fort Utah, is settled by 33 Mormon families in 1849. The name is changed to Provo in 1850.

6 St. George is founded in 1861 by Brigham Young, who sends settlers to the region with instructions to grow cotton there.

3 Travelers on their way to California find gold at Gold Hill in Tooele County in 1858.

N

Scale

0   100 Miles

LEGEND

🏠 Settlement		🥟 Silver	
🎩 Fur		⬜ Utah	
🪨 Gold		— State Border	
— River			

Mormons were the first large group of people from the United States to settle in the Utah region. Led by Brigham Young, many Mormons left Nauvoo, Illinois, after their founder, Joseph Smith Jr., was murdered. They made the 1,000-mile journey to the Great Salt Lake region in 1847 to escape religious **persecution**. The first group of Mormons, including 143 men, three women, and two children, reached the Great Salt Lake valley on July 21, 1847. The Mormons believed Utah was the place to create their own Zion, or kingdom of God. They began to plow and irrigate the land on the day they arrived. They worked the land and built settlements. Spreading out, they created new settlements in neighboring areas. By 1860 about 40,000 Mormons had built more than 150 independent communities.

John C. Frémont's colorful descriptions of the Great Basin encouraged Brigham Young to settle there.

I DIDN'T KNOW THAT!

In 1846 the Donner-Reed expedition traveled by wagon train through Utah on its way to California. The group had to clear a trail through the rough Wasatch Mountains and then cross the salt desert west of the Great Salt Lake. Slowed down by the difficult terrain, the members of the party could not complete their journey before winter, and they were trapped by heavy snow in the Sierra Nevada mountains. Only half of the original party of more than 80 people survived.

In the 1840s, when the beaver trade was declining, mountain men came to the Utah region less often.

In 1857, President James Buchanan, who believed that the Mormons were rebelling against the U.S. government, sent 2,500 soldiers into Utah to replace Governor Brigham Young. The resulting confrontation, which lasted from May 1857 until July 1858, is referred to as the Utah War.

Notable People

Many notable Utahans contributed to the development of their state and country. They include pioneering settlers, scientists and inventors, business leaders, judges, and government officials. Well-known people born in Utah even include one of the most notorious outlaws of the Old West.

**BRIGHAM YOUNG
(1801–1877)**

Born in Vermont, Brigham Young had been a Methodist but converted to Mormonism in 1832. After Mormon leader Joseph Smith Jr. was killed, Young took over as president of the church. He wanted to find a place where his people would be free from religious persecution. He moved them to Utah, which at the time was not part of the United States. After what is now Utah became U.S. land, Young served as the Utah Territory's first governor. He is considered the founder of Salt Lake City.

**BUTCH CASSIDY
(1866–1908)**

Butch Cassidy, born Robert LeRoy Parker, is one of the best-known criminals in American history. He was born into a Mormon family in Beaver. As an adult Cassidy fell in with a sidekick named Harry Longabaugh, nicknamed the Sundance Kid, and a group called the Wild Bunch Gang. Together they organized the longest successful string of train and bank robberies in the history of the American West.

FLORENCE ALLEN (1884–1966)

Florence Allen was born in Salt Lake City. She studied music for many years, but an injury forced her to stop playing the piano. She then began studying law instead. After working as a lawyer, she became a judge. In 1922, she won a seat on the Ohio Supreme Court. She was the first woman to serve on the supreme court of any state.

REVA BECK BOSONE (1895–1983)

Born in American Fork, Reva Beck Bosone taught high school before becoming a lawyer. In 1936, she was elected as a judge in Salt Lake City. Several years later, she became the first woman from Utah to be elected to the U.S. Congress, serving from 1949 to 1953. During her time in Congress, Bosone was an advocate for women and American Indians.

BRENT SCOWCROFT (1925–)

Scowcroft was born in Ogden and attended the United States Military Academy at West Point. He is the founder of The Forum for International Policy and of a consulting firm. In the 1970s and again in the late 1980s and early 1990s, he served as U.S. national security adviser, first under President Gerald Ford and then under President George H. W. Bush.

I DIDN'T KNOW THAT!

Philo Farnsworth (1906–1971) was born near Beaver. He was always interested in physics and chemistry. Farnsworth invented many products over the years, but he is best-known for inventing the first fully electronic television. At the time of this invention, in the 1920s, he was just 21 years old.

John Willard Marriot (1900–1985) was born near Ogden and grew up on a farm. After spending two years working as a Mormon missionary, he opened a chain of restaurants. He eventually expanded the restaurants into hotels. Today, there are more than 3,000 Marriot hotels all over the world.

Population

More than 2.7 million people live in Utah. A sizable majority of Utahans, more than 90 percent, are white. About 12 percent of people who live in Utah claim Hispanic or Latino roots. Hispanic or Latino people can be of any race. More than 75 percent of Utah's residents live along the Wasatch Front, which is a series of valleys and plateaus running along the Wasatch Mountains. Highly populated cities in this area include Salt Lake City, Provo, West Valley City, Sandy, Orem, and Ogden.

Utah Population 1950–2010

Utah is one of the fastest-growing states in the nation. The state's population increased by more than 530,000 people between 2000 and 2010. What factors might contribute to this rapid rate of population growth?

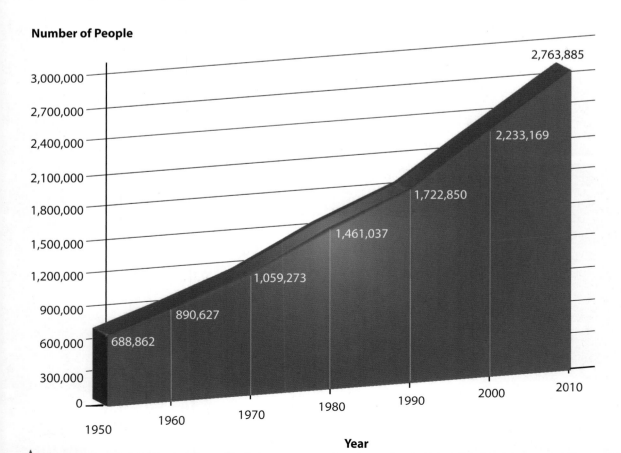

Number of People

- 3,000,000
- 2,700,000
- 2,400,000
- 2,100,000
- 1,800,000
- 1,500,000
- 1,200,000
- 900,000
- 600,000
- 300,000
- 0

688,862
890,627
1,059,273
1,461,037
1,722,850
2,233,169
2,763,885

1950 · 1960 · 1970 · 1980 · 1990 · 2000 · 2010

Year

Utah has an excellent education system. The state has one of the highest **literacy** rates in the United States. In addition, some 88 percent of all Utahans graduate from high school. Utah has a very young population. Nearly one-third of its citizens are under the age of 18. People in this age group make up less than one-quarter of the U.S. population as a whole.

Salt Lake City is part of the Wasatch Front, where most of Utah's residents live.

Only about 9 percent of Utahans are 65 years of age or older. Nationwide, the figure is about 13 percent.

Utah's largest county by population is Salt Lake. Its largest county by size is San Juan.

Utah has one of the highest birth rates among the states, and its death rate ranks among the country's lowest.

Many Utahns live away from the cities in rural areas.

Utah's State Capitol building was constructed between 1912 and 1916. It is open to the public for tours.

Politics and Government

T he Utah state government is divided into three branches. The governor is the head of the executive branch, which also includes the lieutenant governor, treasurer, auditor, and attorney general. Each of these officials is elected to a four-year term.

The legislative branch creates state laws. The Utah legislature includes two chambers, or parts, the Senate and the House of Representatives. The 29 senators serve four-year terms, while the 75 representatives serve two-year terms. The judicial branch of government includes the Supreme Court and eight district courts.

Like all states, Utah is represented in the U.S. Congress in Washington, D.C. Each state elects two U.S. senators, who serve six-year terms. The number of people a state sends to the U.S. House of Representatives is determined by population. Because Utah's population has been growing so rapidly, starting in 2013 the state will have four representatives in the House. This is one more than it had in the previous ten years. U.S. representatives serve two-year terms.

Gary R. Herbert became governor of Utah in 2009. Before that, he had been lieutenant governor for four years.

Cultural Groups

Nearly 60 percent of all Utahans are Mormon, which means that they are members of the Church of Jesus Christ of Latter-day Saints. This church was founded by Joseph Smith Jr. in New York in 1830. The religion's beliefs were explained in *The Book of Mormon*. There are more than 13 million practicing Mormons throughout the world. The headquarters for the Church of Jesus Christ of Latter-day Saints is in Salt Lake City.

The Provo Utah Temple was built in 1911 as part of the Brigham Young University campus.

Rugs woven by Utah's Navajo can be found all over the world.

Smoking and drinking coffee, tea, or alcoholic beverages are prohibited by the Mormon religion.

The Mormon religion places great importance on community and family life. The church community is known to help and support members through difficult times. Mormons strive to dress modestly and to avoid potentially harmful substances such as alcohol. Team sports and other athletic activities are popular with Mormons, who believe in keeping their bodies strong and healthy. The Mormon community also values education and hard work.

Five main American Indian groups live in Utah: the Ute, the Navajo, the Paiute, the Goshute, and the Shoshoni. There are about 3,300 Ute in the state. They have their own tribal government and control about 1.3 million acres of land. There are about 7,000 Navajo, who call themselves Diné, 800 Paiute, and fewer than 500 each of the Goshute and the Shoshoni in the state.

Utah has one of the highest marriage rates in the nation.

Construction of Salt Lake City's Mormon temple began six years after Brigham Young arrived in the region.

Arts and Entertainment

A variety of musicians from Utah have delighted audiences across the nation. The Mormon Tabernacle Choir is a world-famous choir that began in the mid-1800s. Today it has more than 350 singers, who make recordings as well as perform for television and radio broadcasts. Choir members are chosen for their talent and their character. Some choir members are very dedicated, traveling long distances for rehearsals, broadcasts, and other events.

The Mormon Tabernacle Choir has received both Emmy and Grammy Awards.

Both Donnie and Marie Osmond have appeared on Dancing with the Stars.

The Osmonds are a well-known family from Utah. Some of the brothers began performing together in 1957. In the 1960s the Osmond Brothers performed on a variety of popular television shows. One of the brothers, Donny Osmond, began a solo career, became a teen idol, and had numerous Top 40 records. Donny and his sister, Marie, had their own prime-time variety show from 1976 to 1979 and their own talk show in the late 1990s. In 2009, Donny and his partner, Kym Johnson, won first place on *Dancing with the Stars*.

Various festivals are celebrated each year throughout Utah. The Utah Shakespeare Festival, founded in 1961, is held annually in Cedar City. As well as staging four Shakespeare plays every year, the festival has free "Green Shows" before each evening performance. Green Shows feature puppet shows, strolling vendors, musicians, and dancers.

The Festival of the American West is held in Wellsville during the last weekend of July. The fair gives visitors a taste of the Old West, with arts and crafts displays, a cowboy poetry contest, and outdoor performances featuring hundreds of entertainers. People can even witness a re-creation of a rendezvous, with participants dressed up as mountain men.

***American Idol* contestant** David Archuleta grew up in the Salt Lake City suburb of Sandy. In 2010, Archuleta was the guest star at the Mormon Tabernacle Choir Christmas concert.

Ken Jennings is a graduate of Brigham Young University. He holds the record for the longest winning streak on the game show *Jeopardy!*. In 2004, he won 74 games before he was defeated. He earned more than $3 million.

Actor Jason Bateman moved to Salt Lake City when he was four years old. His older sister is *Family Ties* star Justine Bateman.

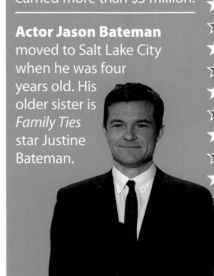

Sports

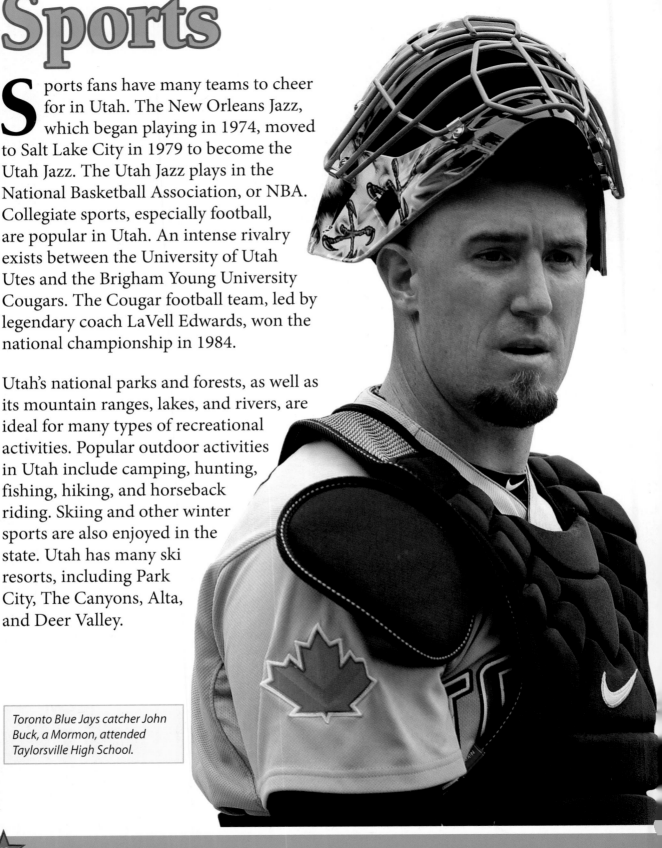

Sports fans have many teams to cheer for in Utah. The New Orleans Jazz, which began playing in 1974, moved to Salt Lake City in 1979 to become the Utah Jazz. The Utah Jazz plays in the National Basketball Association, or NBA. Collegiate sports, especially football, are popular in Utah. An intense rivalry exists between the University of Utah Utes and the Brigham Young University Cougars. The Cougar football team, led by legendary coach LaVell Edwards, won the national championship in 1984.

Utah's national parks and forests, as well as its mountain ranges, lakes, and rivers, are ideal for many types of recreational activities. Popular outdoor activities in Utah include camping, hunting, fishing, hiking, and horseback riding. Skiing and other winter sports are also enjoyed in the state. Utah has many ski resorts, including Park City, The Canyons, Alta, and Deer Valley.

Toronto Blue Jays catcher John Buck, a Mormon, attended Taylorsville High School.

The Utah Jazz play their home games at the EnergySolutions Arena in Salt Lake City. The arena can seat more than 22,000 fans.

Salt Lake City hosted the 2002 Olympic Winter Games, which were held in February. Top athletes from around the world competed in a variety of winter sports, including ski jumping, snowboarding, bobsled, luge, figure skating, and curling.

The venues created for the Olympics are still in use. Children can take part in the Olympic experience through youth sports programs. These programs allow children to participate in and learn about an Olympic sport. The venues are also used for training and development of current and future world-class athletes. Recreational athletes may take advantage of the Olympic facilities as well.

Karl Malone was nicknamed "The Mailman" while a Utah Jazz player because he always "delivered" on the court.

River rafting is a popular sport on Utah's major rivers

American Sara Hughes was only 16 years old when she captured the gold medal in women's figure skating at the 2002 Winter Olympics in Salt Lake City.

Utah has 14 downhill ski resorts. Several of these resorts are less than an hour's drive from Salt Lake City.

National Averages Comparison

The United States is a federal republic, consisting of fifty states and the District of Columbia. Alaska and Hawai'i are the only non-contiguous, or non-touching, states in the nation. Today, the United States of America is the third-largest country in the world in population. The United States Census Bureau takes a census, or count of all the people, every ten years. It also regularly collects other kinds of data about the population and the economy. How does Utah compare to the national average?

Comparison Chart

United States 2010 Census Data *	USA	Utah
Admission to Union	NA	January 4, 1896
Land Area (in square miles)	3,537,438.44	82,143.65
Population Total	308,745,538	2,763,885
Population Density (people per square mile)	87.28	33.65
Population Percentage Change (April 1, 2000, to April 1, 2010)	9.7%	23.8%
White Persons (percent)	72.4%	86.1%
Black Persons (percent)	12.6%	1.1%
American Indian and Alaska Native Persons (percent)	0.9%	1.2%
Asian Persons (percent)	4.8%	2.0%
Native Hawaiian and Other Pacific Islander Persons (percent)	0.2%	0.9%
Some Other Race (percent)	6.2%	6.0%
Persons Reporting Two or More Races (percent)	2.9%	2.7%
Persons of Hispanic or Latino Origin (percent)	16.3%	13.0%
Not of Hispanic or Latino Origin (percent)	83.7%	87.0%
Median Household Income	$52,029	$56,820
Percentage of People Age 25 or Over Who Have Graduated from High School	80.4%	87.7%

*All figures are based on the 2010 United States Census, with the exception of the last two items.

How to Improve My Community

Strong communities make strong states. Think about what features are important in your community. What do you value? Education? Health? Forests? Safety? Beautiful spaces? Government works to help citizens create ideal living conditions that are fair to all by providing services in communities. Consider what changes you could make in your community. How would they improve your state as a whole? Using this concept web as a guide, write a report that outlines the features you think are most important in your community and what improvements could be made. A strong state needs strong communities.

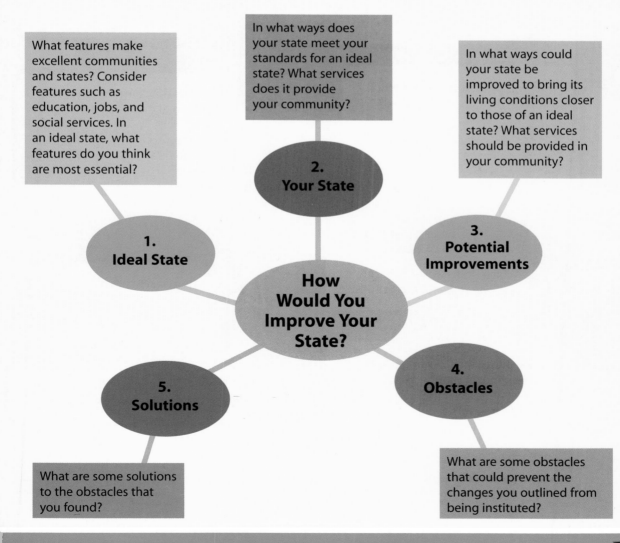

What features make excellent communities and states? Consider features such as education, jobs, and social services. In an ideal state, what features do you think are most essential?

In what ways does your state meet your standards for an ideal state? What services does it provide your community?

In what ways could your state be improved to bring its living conditions closer to those of an ideal state? What services should be provided in your community?

How Would You Improve Your State?

2. Your State

3. Potential Improvements

1. Ideal State

4. Obstacles

5. Solutions

What are some solutions to the obstacles that you found?

What are some obstacles that could prevent the changes you outlined from being instituted?

Exercise Your Mind!

Think about these questions and then use your research skills to find the answers and learn more fascinating facts about Utah. A teacher, librarian, or parent may be able to help you locate the best sources to use in your research.

1 The first department store in the western United States opened up in Utah in 1868. Which store was it?

a) JCPenney
b) Target
c) Zions Cooperative Mercantile Institution (ZCMI)

2 When was the first transcontinental railroad in the nation completed?

a) 1803
b) 1850
c) 1869
d) 1899

3 Which Utah native won *Dancing with the Stars* in 2009?

4 Which one of the following people was not born in Utah?

a) Philo Farnsworth
b) Roseanne Barr
c) Donny Osmond
d) Brigham Young

5 Who was the partner of the legendary Utah-born outlaw Butch Cassidy?

a) Robert Parker
b) Sundance Kid
c) Tonto
d) Miles Goodyear

6 What was the name for the annual gathering of mountain men?

a) rendezvous
b) s'il vous plaît
c) Deseret
d) Paiute

7 How did seagulls help early settlers in Utah?

8 Where is the most productive open-pit copper mine in the world?

Words to Know

annuals: plants that live through only one growing season

birds of prey: birds, such as eagles and hawks, that catch and eat other animals

burrow: a hole dug in the ground in which an animal or animals live

coniferous: trees or shrubs bearing cones and evergreen leaves

diverse: made up of many different elements

endangered: under threat of dying out

expedition: a journey made for exploration

fossil: a rock that contains evidence of an ancient organism, such as a leaf or bone print

irrigation: the supply of water to dry land using pipes, ditches, or streams

literacy: the ability to read and write

mountain ranges: series of connected mountains that are similar in form

Paleo-Indians: prehistoric humans in the Western Hemisphere, believed to have migrated from Asia

paleontologists: people who study prehistoric life by examining early remains and fossils

pelts: skins or hides of animals with the fur still attached

persecution: unfair and cruel treatment of a person or people

poultry: birds, such as chickens, turkeys, ducks, and geese, that are raised for their meat and eggs

prospector: person searching a region for gold or other valuable minerals

transcontinental: extending across a continent

tributaries: streams or rivers that flow into a larger river or other body of water

wholesale: the sale of a large quantity of goods, especially to retail stores

Index

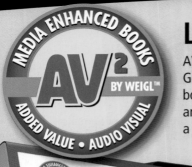

Log on to www.av2books.com

AV² by Weigl brings you media enhanced books that support active learning. Go to www.av2books.com, and enter the special code found on page 2 of this book. You will gain access to enriched and enhanced content that supplements and complements this book. Content includes video, audio, web links, quizzes, a slide show, and activities.

Audio
Listen to sections of the book read aloud.

Video
Watch informative video clips.

Embedded Weblinks
Gain additional information for research.

Try This!
Complete activities and hands-on experiments.

WHAT'S ONLINE?

Try This!	Embedded Weblinks	Video	EXTRA FEATURES
Test your knowledge of the state in a mapping activity.	Discover more attractions in Utah.	Watch a video introduction to Utah.	**Audio** Listen to sections of the book read aloud.
Find out more about precipitation in your city.	Learn more about the history of the state.	Watch a video about the features of the state.	**Key Words** Study vocabulary, and complete a matching word activity.
Plan what attractions you would like to visit in the state.	Learn the full lyrics of the state song.		**Slide Show** View images and captions, and prepare a presentation.
Learn more about the early natural resources of the state.			**Quizzes** Test your knowledge.
Write a biography about a notable resident of Utah.			
Complete an educational census activity.			

AV² was built to bridge the gap between print and digital. We encourage you to tell us what you like and what you want to see in the future.
Sign up to be an AV² Ambassador at www.av2books.com/ambassador.

1

George Lopez

Latino King of Comedy

LILA AND RICK GUZMÁN

Enslow Publishers, Inc.
40 Industrial Road
Box 398
Berkeley Heights, NJ 07922
USA

http://www.enslow.com

Library of Congress Cataloging-in-Publication Data

Guzmán, Lila, 1952-
  George Lopez: Latino king of comedy / Lila and Rick Guzman.
       p. cm.—(Latino biography library)
  Includes bibliographical references and index.
  Summary: "Explores the life of Latino comedian and actor George Lopez, including his childhood and family, his path to success as a comedian, and his charitable work in the community"— Provided by publisher.
  ISBN-13: 978-0-7660-2968-2
  ISBN-10: 0-7660-2968-9
  1. Lopez, George—Juvenile literature. 2. Television actors and actresses—Biography—Juvenile literature. 3. Hispanic American television actors and actresses—Biography—Juvenile literature. 4. Comedians—United States—Biography—Juvenile literature. 5. Hispanic American comedians— Biography—Juvenile literature. I. Guzmán, Rick . II. Title.
  PN2287.L633G92 2009
  791.4502'8092—dc22
  [B]
                                    2007047866

Printed in the United States of America

10 9 8 7 6 5 4 3 2 1

♻ Enslow Publishers, Inc., is committed to printing our books on recycled paper. The paper in every book contains 10% to 30% post-consumer waste (PCW). The cover board on the outside of each book contains 100% PCW. Our goal is to do our part to help young people and the environment too!

To Our Readers: We have done our best to make sure all Internet Addresses in this book were active and appropriate when we went to press. However, the author and the publisher have no control over and assume no liability for the material available on those Internet sites or on other Web sites they may link to. Any comments or suggestions can be sent by e-mail to comments@enslow.com or to the address on the back cover.

Illustration Credits: © ABC/Courtesy Everett Collection, pp. 4, 44, 48, 96; Associated Press, pp. 1, 9, 36, 52, 58, 62, 70, 73, 76, 79, 81, 86; Courtesy of Cedars-Sinai Health System, p. 7; Courtesy Fernie Castillo via Flickr™, pp. 3, 67; Everett Collection, p. 22; Lopez Family, pp. 17, 19, 24, 26, 34; WireImage, p. 99.

Cover Illustration: Associated Press.

Contents

George Lopez prays to God in an episode of _The George Lopez Show_ during its fifth season.

The Secret Patient

"Some people say my wife and I are joined at the hip, but we're really joined at the kidneys!"[1]

—George Lopez

Just before sunrise on April 19, 2005, a couple slipped into Cedars-Sinai Medical Center in Los Angeles, California.[2] The man checked in under the name "Tom Ace." His kidneys were failing and were about to stop making urine. Everyone has two bean-shaped kidneys that clean the blood. They are about the size of a fist and filter waste products.[3] If "Tom Ace" did not get a new kidney soon, he would die.

The secret patient was world-famous comedian and television star George Lopez. He was the star of a hit television sitcom, *The George Lopez Show*. He also performed in comedy clubs around the country and had made several movies. Now he was undergoing surgery to save his life.

Luckily, his wife was a perfect match and could give him a kidney.

No one, not even their closest friends, knew that George and Ann Lopez were going to have surgery.[4] They did not want the press to know about the operation in order to protect their nine-year-old daughter, Mayan. She did not realize how sick her father was, and they did not want her to read about it in the newspaper or see it in a news report on television.

It was a scary time for the Lopez family. George Lopez thought he was going to die, but his wife kept telling him that he was going to be fine.[5] He was afraid he would never see Mayan graduate from high school or get married.

Ann Lopez was not scared to give her husband a kidney and she knew it would save his life. Both her parents were physicians, and she was used to hospitals. She knew how they worked and she knew what to expect when she and her husband went in for surgery.

George Lopez wanted to protect his daughter, but he had another reason for keeping the surgery a secret. Some 170 people worked on his television show and they all had families to support. He worried about how his operation would affect them. He did not want to shut down production of the show. If the show ended because of George Lopez's medical condition, all those people would lose their jobs.

Lopez had his operation at Cedars-Sinai Health System. A statue of Moses is at the entrance to the hospital complex.

On the morning of April 19, 2005, George and Ann Lopez were secretly taken into side-by-side operating rooms in Cedars-Sinai Medical Center. Two surgical teams stood by while George and Ann Lopez were prepped for the operations.

Ann Lopez's surgical team went to work first, putting her under anesthesia. That way she would not be awake during the operation or feel pain.

The surgeon made small cuts about the size of a buttonhole in her skin and inserted a special instrument called an arthroscope. This pencil-sized instrument with a tiny camera attached made parts inside of Ann Lopez's body appear as an image on a television screen. That helped the surgeon harvest one of her kidneys. Harvesting an organ means taking it out so it can be put into someone else's body.

In the meantime, the second surgical team put George Lopez under anesthesia. The last thing he remembered before the operation was seeing a doctor approach and wishing the doctor "Happy Birthday."

When the team was forty-five minutes from harvesting Ann Lopez's kidney, the second surgical team started to operate on George Lopez. They did not take his kidneys out because they were small, about the size of raisins, and would not cause any problems if they stayed in.

Once Ann Lopez's kidney was out, it was whisked to her husband's operating room so it could be put into his body.

The operation was a success so far. But would George Lopez's body accept his wife's kidney? Or would it reject her kidney, and attack it and try to destroy it? They could only wait and see.

George Lopez woke up from surgery and felt "like a hammered sheet of metal."[6] He had never been in more pain. His mouth was dry. With his eyes closed, he listened to the nurses yelling, "Mr. Ace, Tom, wake up!"

George Lopez and wife Ann arrive at the Los Angeles premiere of *Lost City* held at the Cinerama Dome on April 17, 2006 in Hollywood, California. This was only two days before George's kidney operation.

George Lopez thought, "Why are they yelling at this dude, man? Let this guy wake up." Then he realized they were talking to him.

For George Lopez, the funniest part about being in the hospital under an assumed name was the reaction of the man mopping the floor. When someone called George Lopez by his alias, "Tom Ace," the man said, "Hey, *loco*, that's George Lopez."[7]

The night after the operation, Mayan came to the hospital to visit her parents. She missed them a lot. She could not see her father yet, but she saw her mother.

Ann Lopez said that she did not feel any different with one kidney. People can live with only one because kidneys work at only 50 percent each. If one is taken, the other one eventually works at 100 percent.[8]

Both George and Ann Lopez recovered completely from the surgery. Ann Lopez stayed in the hospital for two days and said the procedure was easier than giving birth to a baby. She had a four-inch cut above her belly button and three little scars on the left side that showed where the arthroscopic instruments had gone in.[9] At first, Ann was tired, because it was major surgery and it took about two months for her remaining kidney to take over the work of both kidneys.

Hearing that George Lopez had received a kidney transplant was a surprise to many people. No one knew he was ill, although he had suffered from kidney problems all his life. George Lopez still is not sure why his kidneys started to fail when they did.

After surgery, George Lopez felt incredible, better than he had ever felt in his life. He got better day by day. After a couple of days, when George Lopez's body did not reject the new kidney, the Lopez family knew the operation had been a success. Three weeks after the surgery, he was back on the golf course, playing his favorite game.

> **"I think it was a miracle that my wife's kidney could be used."**

According to the National Kidney Foundation, eighty thousand Americans are waiting for organ transplants. Only fourteen thousand kidney transplants are performed each year. Half the kidneys come from live donors and the other half from dead people.

"It's amazing to be able to help another human being in this way," Ann Lopez said. "You're giving the gift of life."[10]

If someone needs a kidney, it is illegal to buy it. The only way to get one is to have someone give it.[11] That is why organ donation is so important.

"I think it was a miracle," George Lopez said, "that my wife's kidney could be used. Now I value each day because I don't know how long this organ will hold out."[12]

When someone calls Ann Lopez a hero, she shrugs it off. She does not see herself that way. "There was no question," she said. "When you are put in that position where you could possibly lose someone you love, it's a very easy decision."[13] Ann Lopez believes that the real heroes are the people who donate a kidney to someone they do not even know.[14]

No one knows when George Lopez's kidney problems began.[15] When he was a boy, he often wet his bed at night. He never sweated, no matter how hard he played. No one realized that something was wrong with him, not even George Lopez. His doctors think his kidney problems may have started when he was born.[16]

"Why You Crying?"

"I was an only child. I had to share with myself."[1]
—George Lopez, *¡Qué Locos!* television show, Galavisión
Network

George Lopez was born on April 23, 1961, in
Mission Hills, a poor neighborhood in East Los
Angeles, California. He never knew his father, a thin
migrant worker named Anatasio.[2] When George was two
months old, his father left.[3] He took George's birth cer-
tificate and baby clothes. George Lopez still is not sure
why his father did that.

Growing up, George thought his father was dead.
His family told him that, but it may not have been the
truth. Years later, George Lopez would learn that his
father might have been a photographer named
Guzmán. To this day, he has not found him, although he
has looked and looked. He even hired a detective.[4]

For a long time, he wanted to find him, but now he
has given up the search.

After George's father left, he and his mother went to live with her parents, Benita and Refugio Gutierrez. His grandmother was tough and unsympathetic, cold and cruel.[5] Once, when he asked to go to a Chuck E. Cheese restaurant for his birthday, his grandmother said, "You want to see a mouse? Pull the refrigerator out. There are about five Chuckies running around back there."[6]

George Lopez's mother, Frieda, had fallen out of a moving car when she was thirteen years old. From then on, she had epilepsy. Sometimes, all of a sudden, she would fall down and start to jerk violently. George Lopez did not know what to do when she had a seizure. He would scream for help. If no one came, he would stand and watch helplessly until she stopped shaking.

Because of her condition, she did not continue with school and could barely read or write. When she had to sign her name, she wrote an X.

She borrowed money but never paid it back. She liked to go to parties and had a long string of boyfriends. When George was about four years old, a neighbor saw him wandering the streets without any pants on. Once, his mother tried to commit suicide by slashing her wrists. She went to a mental hospital. On Sundays, George would visit her. It made him very sad to see her sedated on drugs, just sitting there. He has no pleasant memories of his mother at all.[7]

George Lopez had a childhood full of poverty and

> **"A life so sad had to be funny."**

14

neglect, but he used those experiences later in his comedy routines. "A life so sad," he said, just "had to be funny."[8] His grandmother, Benita, was the inspiration for many skits in his comedy act and television show. The character Benny on *The George Lopez Show* was based on his grandmother.[9] "Why you crying?" was the line his grandmother used over and over. When George Lopez wrote his autobiography, he titled it *"Why You Crying?"*

He never felt like he belonged. The other children in the neighborhood had brothers and sisters. George Lopez was an only child. He hated his last name because he was the only Lopez in his family. Everyone else was a Gutierrez or a Hernandez.[10]

In spite of all that, he could always make the other children laugh. At first, he thought he was born with a gift for humor. Funny lines would just pop into his head. He later realized that he used that sense of humor to keep from getting hurt.[11]

George grew up speaking Spanglish, a mixture of Spanish and English.[12] Latinos do not speak Spanglish all the time, only when they forget or do not want to use a word in one language or the other.[13] When George Lopez brought a film crew into a writers meeting unexpectedly, he announced to the room: "Sabes que I'm bringing a crew with me."

Spanglish would become an important part of his comedy routine. In his CD *Right Now Right Now*, he said that Latinos speak English and Spanish at the same time and think nothing of it. He gave an example: "Sabes que I went to Walmart and los zapatos that I liked estaban gone."[14]

He has very strong memories of his childhood in East Los Angeles. He was influenced by the Mexican comedian Cantinflas, Mexican soap operas, trips to Mexico, and church. His house was always full of music and he went to see Mexican movies at the local theater.[15]

George did not have a lot of friends. He felt like a nobody. Sometimes parents would not let him play with their children because he was dark-skinned. They even called him bad names. He felt ugly. He thought his head was too big for the rest of his body. His lips felt enormous.[16]

One day, while he played in the school sandbox, a boy about his age joined him. His name was Ernie Arrellano. He and George soon became best friends.[17] They walked to school together, rode bicycles, and watched television. Because they were too poor to buy sports equipment, they learned how to play golf by hitting lemons in the backyard. George would pull the green ones off the tree because they were about the size and shape of golf balls. He used a 7-iron bought at a garage sale. The seller had not used it for golf, but as a weapon in case someone tried to break into the house.

George loved golf. It would become his favorite game. He also loved baseball.

George (in back row, third from left) liked to play Little League baseball. This team picture is from 1973, when he was eleven or twelve years old.

Baseball was his grandfather's favorite game, too. Some of George Lopez's fondest memories are of Friday and Saturday nights at Dodger Stadium with his grandfather. He would eat a hot dog and drink a soda while keeping a Mexican blanket over his lap for warmth. Sometimes, they brought food from home and ate sandwiches or burritos his grandmother had made.[18]

When George got a little bigger, he played Little League.[19] His team practiced and played its games in San Fernando Park. Baseball taught him how to be part of a team. The main lesson he learned was to play in a way that brought out the best in his teammates. He used this skill of teamwork later on *The George Lopez Show.*

George Lopez's grandfather loved road trips to Mexico. He was a big, strong man who worked as a day laborer. Sometimes he worked for two or three weeks straight. Sometimes he was out of work for a while. He was living paycheck to paycheck, but when he went to Mexico, people thought he was rich because he had a house and a car.[20]

In one of his comedy routines, George Lopez recalled a fond memory of his grandfather:

"I remember one time my grandfather put my bike together. There were still parts left. He'd just given up.

"Do it. Mira [Look]. Let's go."

"What are those parts?"

"Don't worry about those. Mira. Go! If it don't work, we'll put some on."

Then you'd be pedaling and the front wheel would come off.

"Ay! That's probably what these are for. Mira . . ."[21]

His grandfather called George "Encanto" meaning "Enchanted." Years later, George Lopez decided to name his production company Encanto Enterprises in honor of the man who taught him how to be a man.[22]

His grandfather was not perfect. He drank alcohol a lot and sometimes hit George and his grandmother. When his grandfather died in 1988 at the age of

George Lopez when he was nine or ten years old in 1971

sixty-three, George Lopez cried for the man who once told him: "I've raised you like my own son. Whatever happens, always remember me. Be a man. Be responsible."[23]

When George was ten years old, his mother married and moved to Sacramento, California. She left George with his grandparents. She later had two girls who are George Lopez's half-sisters. He rarely saw them and does not consider them family.[24]

George's grandmother was never happy, but at least she gave him a home. He knew he was better off with his grandmother, Benita, than with his mother, Frieda, who rarely took care of him.[25]

Abandoning children was an unfortunate tradition in George Lopez's family. His grandmother never knew her mother. When Benita was seven months old, her mother left her with an aunt and went back to Mexico. George's grandmother worked hard, sewing, cleaning and cooking. She was so unhappy, she ran away from home when she was sixteen years old and married a man who beat her.

George Lopez grew up feeling unloved and unwanted. There are no baby pictures of him, no pictures of important events in his life. There are no photos of him until he was seven or eight years old. He never smiled. There was not much to smile about. He never had a birthday party, and he rarely got Christmas presents.[26]

"I never smiled," he said, "because no one made me feel like I was alive. Forget about being important, forget about being a contributing person—no one made me feel like I was alive."[27]

George Lopez remembers seeing a blade of grass growing out of the concrete sidewalk. How did the blade make it through? "That's me," George Lopez said to himself.[28] Although the odds were against him, he was going to make it through the concrete.

A Love for Comedy

"Buenos Días."

> —Freddie Prinze, in the first episode of *Chico and the Man*

Every day after school, George came home to an empty house. His only companion was television. Later, he would say, "In the 70s when I was growing up . . . and I was watching the *Brady Bunch* and the *Partridge Family*, that was the life I wanted."[1] In the summer of 1974, when he was thirteen years old, he saw an ad for a new sitcom. It showed a cool young man named Chico and a '64 Chevy. The ad fascinated George Lopez. He would sit in front of the television just hoping to see the ad again.

When he turned on the TV on Friday, September 13, 1974, he never imagined that a thirty-minute show would change his life forever.

Guitar music and the voice of José Feliciano, a blind Puerto Rican singer and guitarist, filled the room.

Opening credits of a new show, a comedy called *Chico and the Man*, appeared on the screen: "Introducing Freddie Prinze."[2]

George watched, delighted by the show. Set in the barrio of East Los Angeles, the show begins inside a small, run-down garage. An old man named Ed Brown comes down the steps, grumbling and kicking a watering can out of the way. A few minutes later, a young man rides a bicycle into the garage. Chico (played by Freddie Prinze) says, "Buenos días," and tells Ed that he wants to go into business with him. At first, Ed Brown (played

Freddie Prinze acts in a scene with Jack Albertson in the television show *Chico and the Man*.

by actor Jack Albertson, the grandfather in the 1971 movie *Willy Wonka and the Chocolate Factory*) rejects the idea and tells Chico to leave, but that does not stop Chico. Later that night, while Ed Brown is asleep, Chico sneaks into the garage through an open window and cleans up the garage. He moves into an old van. Ed is surprised to see him there when he comes downstairs. By the end of the show, Ed Brown agrees that he needs Chico's help at the garage. Chico is there to stay.[3]

George watched the first episode and then sat back stunned. He had never seen a show like this on television, starring a young Latino comic and sprinkled with a generous amount of Spanish. The only Latino he had seen on television was Pepino on *The Real McCoys*. George was too young to remember *I Love Lucy*. The show starred Lucille Ball and her husband, Desi Arnaz, a Cuban-American musician, actor, television producer, and comedian. It ran from 1951 to 1957 and was the most popular television show of the 1950s.

Seeing Freddie Prinze on *Chico and the Man* changed George Lopez forever. He hung a picture of the young Latino comedian on his bedroom wall. It made him say to himself: "I can be a comedian. I can do what Freddie is doing. I want to make people laugh."[4]

The show became an instant hit, coming in third behind two other comedies, *All in the Family* and *Sanford and Son*. The show soon climbed to number one in the ratings. Freddie Prinze became a household name. So did the things he said, such as "Looooking gooood" and

"Ees not my job." Soon, people everywhere—not just Latinos—were saying those catch phrases.

Every Friday night would find George in front of the television, waiting for *Chico and the Man* to come on. Freddie Prinze was brilliant as Chico Rodriguez, a Mexican American (or Chicano). Freddie Prinze was Latino, like George, but he was not Mexican American, although he played one on the show. He was part Hungarian and part Puerto Rican, whereas George Lopez was Mexican American. Freddie called himself a "Hunga Rican."[5]

Freddie Prinze was a comic genius, but he was only nineteen years old when *Chico and the Man* started. Being successful brought a lot of pressure with it.

Freddie Prinze soon had a drug problem. One night in 1976, he was arrested for driving under the influence of drugs and alcohol.

Chico and the Man was on television from September 1974 to 1978. Before the show ended, on January 28, 1977, Freddie Prinze shot himself while high on drugs. He was rushed to the hospital and died the next day at the age of twenty-two.

George was in the tenth grade at San Fernando High when he heard the news on the radio. He was in shock. His idol was gone. On February 1, 1977, Freddie

George Lopez plays the guitar at the age of sixteen or seventeen in 1978.

Prinze was buried in Forest Lawn Memorial Park, a cemetery where many television and movie stars are buried.[6]

Some people thought the show would be cancelled, but the producers decided to keep going. They introduced a new "Chico." The show was not the same and the network cancelled it the next year.[7]

Freddie Prinze had a profound influence on the comedians who came after him, especially a Mexican-American boy named George Lopez.[8]

Freddie Prinze was gone, but George's dream lived on. He wanted to follow in Freddie's footsteps and make people laugh. In school, he was the class clown. He also had a reputation for being a troublemaker. In the ninth grade, he was arrested because marijuana was found in his locker.

His best friend, Ernie Arrellano encouraged him to become a comedian. He knew someone who was a stand-up comedian. Ernie said, "Man, you're funnier than this dude. Let's go to the clubs and figure out an act.'"[9]

George's family always thought he was wasting his time trying to be a comedian. They never thought he would be anything in life.[10]

Together, George and Ernie hammered out a routine. They worked for hours and hours, day after day. They thought it was perfect and ready for a trial run.

On June 4, 1979, at the age of eighteen, George Lopez went onstage for the first time. It was Open Mic

George Lopez, left, with his best friend Ernie in the 1980s

night at the Comedy Store Annex, a comedy club in Westwood, California, about twenty miles from Lopez's home. "Open Mic" meant that anyone who wanted to perform put a name in a hat. Ten names were pulled out and those ten people would perform. That night, George Lopez got lucky. His name was drawn.

George Lopez was scared to stand onstage in front of forty or so people. Somehow he managed to do the comedy routine that he and Ernie had worked out.

No one laughed. It was an awful experience. Being a stand-up comic was hard, George Lopez realized. He was not born with this talent. Someone could not teach him. He had to learn on his own.[11] And it would to take a lot of practice.

In the meantime, on August 6, 1979, George Lopez graduated from San Fernando Valley High School. He had failed English during the regular school year and had to go to summer school. Still, he became the first person in his family to graduate from high school.

A few days after getting his diploma, he wrote a promise to himself. "I will hit the American people like a hammer. I will be the best."[12] It would take him more than twenty years to keep that promise.

Lopez started working a string of jobs that he hated. One job was for a book company. He got $2.35 an hour to take orders, fill boxes, and ship them to customers. After he got fired from that job, he went to a trade school to learn about electronics. He got a job making floppy discs for computers, but that did not work out. He moved on to Sperry Aviation, where he worked alone, at night, testing circuit boards. Working in an airplane parts factory was an experience that would later become the foundation for his television show.[13]

Lopez did not like any of these jobs because, deep down, he wanted to be a stand-up comedian. He and Ernie came up with new jokes and tried to improve the comedy routine. They spent their free time writing and polishing comedy bits—and partying. Sometimes, after a performance, they would go get hamburgers and talk about how the show went and how to make it better.

Occasionally, Ernie Arrellano recorded the routine and played it back later.

After three years with Sperry Aviation, George Lopez was laid off when the company moved to Arizona. For the next two years, he assembled computers. His pay went up to eight dollars an hour. He continued to live with his grandparents and felt all his jobs had no future. Finally, he decided it was time to get serious about his comedy career.

Lopez quit his job. On July 17, 1987, at the age of twenty-six, he set out. He traveled from club to club around the Los Angeles area. For a year, he did his act in small comedy clubs before he was able to move up to better places. One night, after he performed at the Improv on Melrose, Arsenio Hall came up to him and told him he wanted him to appear on his new talk show. George Lopez was overjoyed. Hall had one of the coolest shows on television.

> *Finally, Lopez decided it was time to get serious about his comedy career.*

After that, George Lopez frequently appeared on *The Arsenio Hall Show*. He also performed on *Comic Strip Live*, *Evening at The Improv*, and *The Tonight Show With Johnny Carson*.[14]

In his comedy routine, George Lopez joked about Latino culture and talked about the differences between Latinos and Anglos.[15] He also talked about current events.

During this time, he met Constance Marie, an actress. They did not have an act planned out, but they did twenty minutes of comedy. To their surprise, they found that they worked well together. They were both frustrated by Hollywood and the lack of good roles for Latinos. They were disappointed by the kinds of roles they were offered. Together, they came up with an idea for a television series about a Latino couple. It would be a Latino *Honeymooners* based on the popular television show in the 1950s. In *The Honeymooners*, Jackie Gleason played a bus driver who lived with his sharp-tongued but loving wife in Brooklyn.

The idea of a Latino *Honeymooners* never went anywhere, but later when it came time to find an actress to play his wife on *The George Lopez Show*, Constance Marie was the natural choice. She was delighted with the new project. The scripts were thought-provoking and funny. She found the show a refreshing change from the negative stereotypes of Latinos on TV and in the movies.[16]

However, in early 1990, although he worked hard to be a success and found a lot of jobs, Lopez's career seemed stuck. He did not make much money. He felt like giving up.

Then, one night, he met the person who would change his life forever. In May 1989, a woman named Ann Serrano came into The Ice House Comedy Club in Pasadena, California. It is the oldest stand-up comedy club in the United States.[17] Many famous comedians had performed there: Jay Leno, Jerry Seinfeld, Lily

Tomlin, Bob Newhart, George Carlin, David Letterman, Billy Crystal, Steve Martin, Rosie O'Donnell, Dana Carvey, Robin Williams, Dennis Miller, and Bill Maher.[18]

All the seats at the Ice House are within seven rows of the stage. George Lopez noticed a woman in the audience. It was not love at first sight. There were no fireworks. After the show, they introduced themselves and started talking. Most of the conversation was about the lack of Latinos on TV and in the movies. She asked him to perform at a comedy fundraiser she was organizing.[19]

He accepted. George Lopez did not know it at the time, but he had just met his future wife.

George and Ann Lopez

GEORGE LOPEZ: She threw me out of the house. That will get your attention.
ANN LOPEZ: Never cross a Cuban woman.[1]

> —Ann and George Lopez on *Larry King Live*

Ann Serrano was not Mexican American like George Lopez. She was a first-generation Cuban American born in Hartford, Connecticut. Her parents, both medical doctors, worked at a hospital there. Her mother, father, sister, and grandmother had left Cuba with nothing but two bags, eight hundred dollars, family pictures, and their wedding rings. Like many Cubans, they came to the United States after the revolution in 1959.

Before Ann Serrano met George Lopez at the Ice House, she saw him on tape. As a casting assistant at Disney, her job was to find talented Latino comedians. She did a national search, but found only disappointment. Then, she saw a tape of George Lopez performing. She liked his comedy and thought it was honest, without being mean. Then she saw him onstage and liked him even more.

Lopez's act was not perfect, but Ann believed he would become a great comedian.[2] She could see that he tried hard and wanted to do better. She liked that because she was from a culture that valued hard work.[3]

Lopez began making a name for himself in Southern California on the comedy circuit. He performed fifteen times on *The Arsenio Hall Show*, more times than any other comedian. He did a lot of television stand-up comedy shows: *Comic Strip Live*, *Sunday Comics*, *VH1 Comedy Hour*, *MTV's Half Hour Comedy Hour*, *Evening at the Improv*, and many others. But he wanted more. He did not want to be a good comedian. He wanted to be a great one. He was frustrated.

Ann Serrano became his manager and publicist. That meant sending out letters and tapes to places looking for comedians and calling casting directors and other contacts to let them know about George Lopez.

She got him some impressive jobs. He performed the opening act for Bob Hope, a famous comedian and actor, and Ray Charles, a famous singer. George Lopez got lots of television airtime. Still, people saw him as a Latino comedian, and George Lopez did not like that. He did not want to be labeled.

After a couple of years of dating George Lopez, Ann Serrano was ready to get married. In December 1992, she saw that Lopez was not going to pop the question, so she did it herself.

"Guess who's getting married?" she asked him one day.

"Who?"

"Us," she replied.

"Really? When?"

"Next September."

"All right, let me know. I'll be there."[4]

It was very unromantic, she said. He did not take her to a fancy restaurant and get down on one knee to ask her to marry him. She even had to buy her own ring.[5]

They married on September 18, 1993. Because they are both Roman Catholics, they decided to have the ceremony at the San Fernando Mission in San Fernando, California. Their daughter, Mayan, was born three years later.

Their marriage was bumpy at first, and Lopez blames himself for their problems. He felt that he did not deserve to be loved. "I didn't know how to love because I didn't see any good examples of it," he said.[6] He credits Ann Lopez with saving him from himself. She was the first person to ever love him unconditionally.[7]

> "I didn't know how to love because I didn't see any good examples of it."

Because his parents were not around and he was raised by a cruel grandmother, George Lopez did not

George Lopez and Ann Serrano were married on September 18, 1993.

know what love felt like. Ann had to teach him that it was okay to love and be loved in return.[8]

One Valentine's Day after his television show had started, as a gift, Ann took George's old high school baseball varsity letter that he tucked away in a drawer and had it sewn on a varsity jacket. Years earlier, when he first earned the letter, his grandmother had refused to buy a jacket for him. Ann gave the jacket to him at the studio where they filmed his show. George Lopez started to put it on. Before he got both arms in the sleeves, he began to cry. "Bawling my eyes out right there on Sound Stage 4, overwhelmed by an act so thoughtful and kind, symbolic of a healthy family relationship— wife, husband, and child—I'd never known except on TV."[9]

However, before this incident, for several years after George and Ann married, he felt that his career was going nowhere. He played small parts in movies. His first major film role had been in 1990 when he played "Eddie" in *Ski Patrol*.[10] Three years later, he played a murder investigator in the comedy movie *Fatal Instinct*.

Once in a while, he turned down a movie role if it was a part that made Latinos look bad.[11] He refused to play certain roles, although it would have helped his career. He turned down a part in *Desperado*, a 1995 movie starring Antonio Banderas, because he did not want to play a drug dealer and a gang member. He felt those roles did not represent most Latinos, and he did not want people to think that all Hispanics were bad guys. Instead, he looked for roles that would show them in a good light. In his later movies, he would play teachers, FBI agents, and other role models.

Lopez continued to work at stand-up comedy. He would spend three or four days with his wife. The weekend would come, and he would hit the road again. His life seemed humdrum. He got tired of traveling, living in motel rooms, and eating at fast-food restaurants.[12] He got to the point that he simply did not like his life or himself.[13]

George Lopez, his wife Ann, and daughter Mayan arrive at Nickelodeon's 20th Annual Kids' Choice Awards held at Pauley Pavilion on March 31, 2007 in Westwood, California. Mayan was born in 1996.

Ann Lopez made excuses for him because of his awful childhood. But one night, when Mayan was just a baby, Ann had had enough. George had been drinking too much and staying out late. She decided it was time for some tough love. She kicked George out of the house. In the middle of the night, she crammed his car with his clothes, razor, toothbrush, toothpaste, a frying pan, and toilet paper. She said to herself: "Buddy, you're not coming back." Then, she changed the locks.[14]

George Lopez got into his Volvo. It was packed with so much of his stuff, he could barely shift the car into gear. He went to the condo they had lived in before they bought a house. There was no furniture except for Mayan's crib left behind when they moved. He lived in the condo for a month, sleeping on a rollaway bed, feeling miserable. Seeing his daughter's empty crib night after night made him realize that he was blowing his chance to have a normal family. At that point, he made an important decision. He would turn his life around. He went home. He and his wife had a long talk and made up. She told him, "That's it. You've had your mid-life crisis, you've had your fifties crisis, you've had your sixties crisis, your seventies crisis and you can't have any more."[15]

They started going to therapy to work out their problems. Going to a marriage counselor helped George Lopez learn how to talk openly and honestly about his past.

Describing George, Ann said, "You know, George just had a horrible childhood and . . . he never saw people who loved each other. He never saw people who respected each other. He never really saw family. They never celebrated birthdays or Christmas very much. So . . . I don't think he could accept the life I was trying to give him, which was a very traditional marriage, a very traditional life, and he was fighting it . . . At home, he'd be a great husband and a great father and then he'd go on the road and he was drinking, drinking a lot."[16]

Over the years, the Lopezes were able to build a strong, healthy relationship. George Lopez is completely devoted to his family now and has made a promise in public never to make his wife unhappy again.[17]

Enter Sandra Bullock

"Outside of Ann, I owe everything to Sandy because she didn't have to do this."[1]

—George Lopez

Therapy helped George Lopez work through the demons of his childhood. Growing up abandoned and unloved nearly destroyed his marriage and his life. Once he cleaned up his act, good things started happening.[2] He signed a contract with Ron De Blasio, one of the best agents in Hollywood, who once had managed Freddie Prinze's career.

Ron De Blasio had managed other big names in comedy—Bill Cosby, George Carlin, Richard Pryor, and others. After Freddie Prinze's death, De Blasio decided he could not work with comedians any more. He signed only musicians. But when he met George Lopez, he knew he was different somehow. He felt Freddie Prinze's presence when he was with Lopez. De Blasio said: "I felt like this was probably the extension of what Freddie and I were going to do."[3]

George Lopez had the same feeling: Freddie was a guardian angel watching over him. Lopez's confidence grew and grew and his comedy act got better and better.[4]

De Blasio's hard work soon paid off. Bigger and better clubs hired George Lopez. He began to make a name for himself. In 2001, he hosted a morning radio program. He was the first Latino to star on an English-language station in Los Angeles.[5]

The same year, the movie *Bread and Roses* came out. It told the story of janitors going on strike in Los Angeles. George Lopez played the heroine's sleazy boss. The main character, Maya, is an illegal immigrant in Los Angeles who works as a low-paid janitor in very bad working conditions.[6] Her boss mistreats her and bullies her and other workers when they try to form a union. In spite of all his threats and abuse, the workers win.[7]

The movie was very well received at the Cannes Film Festival, held once a year in southern France. George Lopez could not believe it. "This abused, neglected kid," he later wrote, "who hated the color of his skin, who found quiet comfort in television, was headed to Cannes."[8] The movie won the Phoenix Award at California's Santa Barbara International Film Festival.

In Real Women Have Curves (2002), the main character is a girl who is not slim but is happy with her size. She knows she is beautiful on the outside and on the inside. Ana, a first generation Mexican-American teenager, is played by America Ferrera. Many people now know her as the star of the television show *Ugly Betty*. In *Real Women Have Curves*, Ana could get a college scholarship, but her family—especially her mother—stands in the way. She makes Ana work in the dress factory run by Ana's sister. The days are long and the pay is poor.

George Lopez plays her high school teacher, Mr. Guzmán, who hates to see her sacrifice her future out of duty to her family. Ana has to decide between her family and education. She leaves home and goes to college. The movie won an Audience Award at the 2002 Sundance Film Festival in Utah.[9]

By now, George Lopez had been on the comedy circuit for more than fifteen years. Then, one night at the Improv, his life changed completely. A famous actress named Sandra Bullock entered his life.

She had starred in a number of hit movies—including *Speed*, *While You Were Sleeping*, and *Miss Congeniality*—and now had her own production company. She and her business partner, Jonathon Komack Martin, were putting together some television projects and noticed there were no shows starring Latinos or Asians. James Komack, Jonathan's father, had been the producer of *Chico and the Man* in the 1970s. Bullock and Martin wondered why *Chico and the Man* had been the last successful Latin sitcom. Why weren't there more Latinos on TV? Bullock decided to change that because she loves the Latino culture.[10]

Bullock and Martin agreed that they wanted to do a Latino show and began to hunt for talent. Then Bullock found George Lopez. When she saw his act, she knew he had great potential. She liked his edgy comedy, his honesty, and the way he made people think in new directions.[11] One night after a show, she talked to Lopez and told him his act would make a great television series. He agreed.

The next problem was to find the right vehicle for the show. Bullock had been looking for ideas for a show. A writer had pitched the "Latino Beverly Hillbillies" to her, but it did not feel right. Maybe, she thought, a show about Latino teenagers would work. They would be the stars of the show and their parents would be secondary characters.

Many of the people Bullock worked with did not think a show about Latinos would work. They told her not to do it, but she did not listen to their advice. Instead, she talked to Bruce Helford, an important man in the entertainment industry. He had been the head writer for *Roseanne* (1988–1997) and had created *The Drew Carey Show* (1995–2004).[12] He liked Bullock's idea and decided it would work. He became the show's co-creator and executive producer.

Then they had to find the cast. Because there had not been a successful Latino comedy since *Chico and the Man* in the 1970s, there had not been a big demand for Latinos in television. Some had been in serious roles. Jimmy Smits had starred in *L.A. Law*. Hector Elizondo

The Cast of *The George Lopez Show*

The actors who play George Lopez's TV family are:

Constance Marie—George Lopez's wife, Angie

Belita Moreno—his mother, Benny

Masiela Lusha—his daughter, Carmen

Luis Armand Garcia—his son, Max

(Aimee Garcia was added as Veronica, George Lopez's niece in Season Six. Emiliano Diez joined the cast as his Cuban father-in-law, Vic Palmero.)

was in *Chicago Hope*. Benjamin Bratt had played a New York City detective in *Law and Order*.

The pool of known Latino talent for a comedy show was much smaller than Bullock and Helford expected. They thought they might have to go to Mexico City for actors.[13] They posted a casting call in the trade papers that actors and agents read. The ad gave a brief description of the sitcom and the characters and their ages. Lots of actors showed up to try out for the parts. Bullock and Helford found a very talented cast in the United States.[14] Everyone they hired was Latino except for Masiela Lusha, an actress who was born in Albania.

From left to right is the cast of *The George Lopez Show*: Belita Moreno, Valente Rodriguez, Luis Armand Garcia, Masiela Lusha, Emiliano Diez, Constance Marie, and George Lopez.

Each week, the audience sees what the family goes through in their day-to-day lives. George Lopez based the show on experiences from his own life. He plays the manager of an airplane parts factory in Los Angeles. He has a best friend named Ernie, just like his best friend from childhood, and a mother, Benny, based on his grandmother. Lopez's TV mother works at the airplane factory, too. When Lopez worked for Sperry Aviation in the 1980s, his grandmother worked as an inspector there.[15] Angie, his television wife, is Cuban-American, just like his wife, Ann Lopez. In real life, George Lopez has a daughter named Mayan. On the show, he has two children: Carmen and Max.[16]

Everything was in place. ABC bought only four episodes, because a new show was always risky. Lopez's show would start in March, at the end of the television season. Filming of *The George Lopez Show* began at Warner Brothers Television on Sound Stage 4.

George Lopez was not accustomed to acting on television. He had no idea how different it was from stand-up comedy. On stage, he had to use wild hand motions and facial expressions. He ran across the stage, pretended to fall down, and danced around the microphone stand. He bugged out his eyes and used "barrio speak" that included lots of bad words. Performing on television was exactly the opposite. Lopez had to stop bugging out his eyes and playing it big.[17]

One day, one of the actors showed up unprepared and had not memorized the lines. George Lopez got very upset. Bruce Helford had to pull the actor aside and explain: "You don't *understand*. This is his *life*."[18]

Lopez knew that this was his chance to make it big. He did not want anything or anyone messing it up. He understood the enormous responsibility he had to the cast and crew. He was not just the star of the show. He was the co-creator and a writer and producer, too. Everyone working on the show was his "family" and he took his role as the head of the family very seriously.[19]

The first show aired on March 27, 2002. Everyone seemed on edge, waiting to see how the show would do.

Would the public like it? What would the critics say? If those four episodes did not bring in good ratings, ABC would not buy more episodes. The show would be cancelled.

George Lopez had to wait until August to learn what ABC had decided. He was in a car on his way to a comedy club in Houston, Texas, when his cell phone rang. It was Bruce Helford calling from Warner Brothers. He had just heard from executives at ABC. The show had done well enough to be on the fall schedule. The network bought thirteen episodes.[20]

Lopez was overjoyed! He could not believe it.

The second season began in October 2002. *The George Lopez Show* became the most watched show in its time slot. About twelve million viewers tuned in each week. Most were not Latino; Lopez wanted it that way. Too many people, Lopez knew, saw Latinos as the people who took care of other people's kids, cut the grass, and cooked their food. He wanted them to realize that Latinos are just regular people, not stereotypes.[21]

A network executive called him to complain about the kitchen on the set. "George Lopez," he said, "there's nothing in the kitchen that tells anybody that a Mexican family lives there." He wanted to put in a tortilla maker.

A tortilla maker? Lopez did not know what that was. His grandmother had been his tortilla maker. Lopez told the executive that Mexicans in the kitchen told the viewers that it was a Mexican kitchen.

George Lopez wanted his show to be different. The characters did not spit out Spanish when they got mad. When they raised their voices, they spoke English. In the first show, there was only one word of Spanish.[22]

To boost ratings in the second season, Sandra Bullock volunteered to guest-star for four weeks during the November ratings sweep. She played "Accident Amy," a clumsy worker in the factory that Lopez manages.

It worked! The show moved up even more in the ratings. Soon, it was in the top twenty-five shows. That meant even more people all across the country were watching it.[23]

Then, one day, George Lopez got another phone call from ABC. The voice on the line said: "George Lopez, I just wanted to tell you we've picked up the show for the back nine."

The back nine! That meant that ABC had committed to an entire season of twenty-two episodes. That also meant that *The George Lopez Show* was the most successful Latino family sitcom in television history. It also became the top-rated sitcom on ABC.[24]

> *There were tears in Lopez's eyes as he hung up the phone.*

There were tears in Lopez's eyes as he hung up the phone. He could barely control himself as he made his way back to the set of the show. He called the entire cast and crew together and told

Sandra Bullock helped get *The George Lopez Show* off the ground. She even appeared in four episodes during Season 2, playing a character called "Accident Amy."

them that ABC wanted nine more episodes. They jumped for joy when they heard the news.

The network executives at ABC were happy as well. ABC had taken a big risk and it had paid off. Each episode cost more than two hundred fifty thousand dollars to make. The budget for a typical season was more than $30 million. About 125 people worked on the show. Besides the actors, there were many people who worked behind the scenes: carpenters, painters, hair stylists, makeup artists, set designers, and others.[25]

George Lopez gave Sandra Bullock a lot of credit for the show's success. "I owe everything to her, because she didn't have to do this."[26]

For years, Lopez had worked hard to become a success. And now he had achieved it.

The George Lopez Show

"I don't know why you married a Cuban anyway. They eat bananas and coconuts. Those people eat like they're shipwrecked."[1]

—"Benny" on *The George Lopez Show*

George Lopez's success came as the result of years of hard work. And it was not over yet. Filming each episode of his show proved just as difficult. Filming came at the end of a long week for the cast and crew of about 170 people.

Here is a typical schedule for filming *The George Lopez Show*:

Monday: The week starts with a production meeting. The cast, executives, producers, writers, and department heads gather in a big room for a Table Read. They sit around a big table and read every line of the script. Then, they discuss it. They talk about the clothes the actors will wear, what the set will look like for the show, where the cameramen will shoot it, and other technical matters.[2] After the production meeting, the actors rehearse for the rest of the day.

Tuesday: Everyone rehearses for three hours in the morning and two hours in the afternoon. Then there is a network/studio run-through. Network and show executives, writers, agents, friends, and family watch the show. The executives then give notes to make it better. The writers and actors work until seven or eight o'clock, sharpening scenes and lines.

Wednesday: Camera blocking begins. During this process, the director figures out where the actors should stand on stage and where they will move during a scene. Besides five more hours of rehearsal, Lopez runs lines with his acting and dialogue coaches. He has to memorize scripts that are forty or more pages. "Laughers" show up. They get free food and coffee as their reward for sitting hour after hour and laughing on cue.[3]

Thursday: This is Show Day. The show is rehearsed on a closed set. That means there is no audience. Around 5 P.M., the actors get their hair and make-up done. They put on the clothes they are going to wear for the show. They get final notes and changes in the script.[4] At 5:25 P.M., the cast comes out and meets a live audience. George Lopez grabs the mike and does a little comedy routine. He brings someone on stage with him. Sometimes it is one of the crew. Sometimes, it is an audience member. After three-and-a-half hours of shooting, there is enough film for the television show. It has to be edited down to exactly twenty-two minutes

Actor George Lopez speaks to the live audience as cast members, Valente Rodriguez, (second from left), Luis Armand Garcia and Masiela Lusha, (right), watch on the set of *The George Lopez* Show on September I, 2005, in Burbank, California.

long.[5] When commercials and other material are added, it will be thirty minutes long.

All episodes of *The George Lopez Show* began with his signature song, "Low Rider" by the band War. Each time he stepped on the set to film an episode, Lopez slid a leather key ring into his right pants pocket. The key ring is a good luck charm because it once belonged to Freddie Prinze. Kathy Prinze, his widow, gave it to Lopez.[6]

The show remained popular because the on-screen family faced similar problems to those of regular off-screen families. Carmen, George Lopez's TV daughter, dealt with issues that any normal teenage girl faced: dating, problems at school, dealing with her parents.[7] Her reputation was damaged when an angry ex-boyfriend spread false rumors about her. Another time, George Lopez taught Carmen how to drive. The actress who played Carmen left the show after the fifth season. To explain her absence, the show's writers had her character, Carmen Lopez, go to college in another town.

In one show, Max learns that he has dyslexia, a learning disorder that makes it difficult for a person to learn to read. People with dyslexia are just as smart as everyone else, but they read at lower levels. They have special needs and learn in different ways from other students. On the TV show, Lopez admits to his family that he is dyslexic in order to help his son cope with his problem.[8]

One episode dealt with steroids. The performance-enhancing drug had been in the news before the show aired. There was a lot of discussion about professional baseball and football players using steroids. Bruce Helford, the executive producer of the show, said he did not like "issue shows," but he became aware of the steroid problem when his twelve-year-old son was playing Little League. It seemed that everyone wanted to "bulk up" and use supplements.[9] Helford hopes that families will see the show and will discuss steroids. "If one parent talks to one kid and discusses this intelligently, that's fantastic," he said. "One of the wonderful

An Award-Winning Show

Between its premiere in March 2002 and its cancellation in May 2007, *The George Lopez Show* was nominated for numerous awards and brought home several trophies. It won the following:

2003

- Image Award for Best Primetime Comedy Series – Television
- Award from the American Society of Composers, Authors and Publishers (ASCAP) for "Top TV Series"
- Young Artist Award for "Best Family Television Series (Comedy or Drama)"
- 2003 and 2004 Young Artist Award for "Best Performance in a TV series – Leading Young Actress" (Masiela Lusha)

2004

Image Awards for:

- Best Actor in a Television Comedy (George Lopez)
- Best Actress in a Television Comedy (Constance Marie)
- Best Primetime Series – Comedy
- Best Supporting Actress in a Television Comedy

2005

- Emmy (Art director and set director)

things about a sitcom is you are laughing along with it. It can be effective without being preachy."[10]

Some of the shows are based on events from George Lopez's life. Over the years, the television show and his comedy routine have helped him work out painful issues of his childhood.

In one episode, George Lopez set out to find his father when he learned that he was actually alive. In another, the issue of divorce came up when Angie learned that her parents were getting divorced after many years of marriage. Some of the shows were light-hearted, such as going on a trip to Disneyland. Some are more serious, such as focusing on an alcohol problem or being overweight.

One episode was based on Lopez's kidney problem when he was a child. His on-screen son, Max, had to have an operation to avoid kidney disease in the future.[11]

As a fictional father, George Lopez's character ranked Number 18 in *TV Guide's* list of the "Fifty Greatest TV Dads of All Time."[12] George Lopez believes people like him and the show because "I'm a real person, a regular guy with all the nicks and cuts of anyone who has struggled to get by."[13]

To come up with story ideas for the show, George Lopez regularly met with a team of about twelve writers. Some on his writing staff were not Latinos, so they did not know how to write ethnic material. George Lopez often told them stories from his youth, such as using a fork to roast hot dogs on the stove. "Just write me funny," he told them. "I'll be the barometer of what is ethnic and what is not."[14] Bruce Helford, his producer, added, "When it comes to . . . things that are specific to Hispanic culture, George is on top of that."[15]

The show's popularity took Lopez to places he never expected to go. In March 2003, George Lopez found

Honors for George Lopez

The George Lopez Show has been nominated for so many awards. Likewise, George Lopez has been flooded with awards for his accomplishments in the entertainment industry and for his charitable work. He has received:

- Latino Spirit Award for Excellence in Television

- The National Hispanic Media Coalition Impact Award

- The Manny Mota Foundation Community Spirit Award

- Honorary Mayor of Los Angeles (for raising funds for earthquake victims in El Salvador and Guatemala)

- The 2004 Artist of the Year and Humanitarian Award (Harvard University)

- 2004 Spirit of Liberty Award (People for the American Way)[16]

himself performing for President George W. Bush and his wife, Laura, in the historic Ford Theatre in Washington, D.C.,[17] the place where Abraham Lincoln was assassinated in 1865.

For George Lopez, it was a once-in-a-lifetime moment and he was very nervous. He started telling jokes and his confidence grew when he saw President and Mrs. Bush laughing and having a good time.

"Someday soon," George Lopez said, "there's going to be a Latino in the White House. Of course, we plan on leaving it white . . . with just a little blue trim."[18]

At the end of the show, the Navy Choir joined Lopez and the other performers on stage—R&B singer and songwriter Brian McKnight, country music singer LeAnn Rimes, and actress Michele Lee, star of the popular television show *Knots Landing*. They began to sing. When they were finished, President Bush came up to the podium to thank everyone and give a short speech.

George Lopez was now a foot and a half away from "the Man."[19] He thought: "This is probably the closest any Chicano I know has ever got to this kind of power without saying, 'More coffee, Mr. President?'"[20] He was so close, he could see his name written on the President's speech.

The President thanked everyone and left. More importantly, he left the speech on the podium. It was too much of a temptation. George Lopez knew it would make a nice souvenir. When no one was looking, he took it and put it in his pocket. Then he got into the limo

Presenter George Lopez jokes as he takes the stage during the 32nd Annual People's Choice Awards in Los Angeles, on January 10, 2006.

with his wife to go to a party. He did not know that all presidential papers, even a speech left behind on a podium, would eventually go to a presidential museum.

He did not think anyone had seen him take the speech . . . but someone had. At the party, a Secret Service agent, one of the guards for the President, approached George Lopez. "Mr. Lopez," he said, "I'm from the Secret Service, and we'd like to speak with you."

George Lopez confessed before the man actually accused him of stealing the speech. Surprised and embarrassed, he went out to the limo and got it. He asked the agent how he knew he had stolen the speech.

When it turned up missing, the agent explained, the Secret Service went to the TV production truck and watched the videotape of the show. They went through it scene-by-scene until they saw George Lopez slip the speech into his pocket.[21]

"You know," the Secret Service agent said, "my money was on Michele Lee."

The incident inspired an episode for *The George Lopez Show* when the third season started. "Dubya, Dad, and Dating" aired on September 26, 2003. The President visits the airplane parts factory where George Lopez works and gives a speech. Afterwards, the Secret Service shows up at Lopez's house and accuses him of stealing the speech. But in this version, George Lopez did not take it.

Most of the episodes of *The George Lopez Show* avoided politics. "Dubya, Dad, and Dating" was an exception.

Red-hot topics such as the immigration issue were deliberately kept out of the show. In Southern California, the topic generates a lot of passion. The cast and crew worked together like a happy family. George Lopez wanted to keep it that way.[22]

But he does not avoid controversy when he does comedy in a club. "I have an ability to say things most people get in trouble for," he says. "I've got to speak out."[23] A few years ago, someone suggested that the United States build a canal on the Mexican border and fill it with alligators to keep illegal immigrants out. "Go ahead," George Lopez said, knowing that hardworking immigrants would see it as an opportunity. "In three weeks, you'd have people selling (alligator) belts and wallets."[24]

"America's Mexican"

"People ask me, does it matter if someone calls you a Mexican, Latino, or Hispanic? I don't mind Mexican or Chicano, which is a Mexican American, but Hispanic I don't like . . . Who wants to be associated with a word that has *panic* in it?[1]

—George Lopez

The George Lopez Show was a good, solid show, but never a smash hit. Even so, it did well against the very popular *American Idol*. In some markets (San Antonio, for example), it even beat *Idol* in ratings.[2]

About seven million viewers watched Lopez's show each week.[3] America obviously loved the show and Lopez became, in his own words, "America's Mexican."[4]

The George Lopez Show was the first successful show in the history of television with a Mexican-American actor as the star. It was also the first successful Latino comedy since *Chico and the Man* in the 1970s.[5] In 1984, Paul Rodriguez had a sitcom called *a.k.a. Pablo* but it did not last long.[6] George Lopez once remarked: "Desi Arnaz,

Freddie Prinze and I are in a club that only has three members."[7]

Although *The George Lopez Show* was based on his early life, he has not stayed in contact with people from that sad time. His mother is alive, but he does not talk to her. In the early 1990s, George Lopez and Ernie Arrellano went their separate ways after an argument over money. For ten years, they did not speak, but eventually they patched up their differences and see each other from time to time.[8] George Lopez's grandfather died in 1988, but his grandmother is still alive. He sees

George Lopez takes a break on the set of *The George Lopez Show* at Warner Brothers Studios in Burbank, California, on August 22, 2006.

her from time to time. She now has dementia, a kind of mental illness.[9]

Nowadays, George Lopez looks at his early life as a closed chapter in a book.

Sometimes people criticize him because he makes a lot of money talking about his family. "I didn't ask for them to treat me the way they treated me," he responds. "I'm just reporting the facts."[10] For George, his wife and daughter are his family, along with his fans.[11]

The cast and crew are also like family to him. Over the years, props were added to the set that hold great sentimental value for George Lopez. Most viewers do not look closely at the objects around the set and would not notice two jerseys on the wall of the sports bar that the show's characters go to from time to time. The shirts read "Hanson" and "Johnson" and they hang next to Artis Gilmore's basketball jersey.

They were there as a way to honor two young women who played soccer on the National Select Team of the United States Adult Soccer Association. Twenty-year-old Jessica Hanson, her father, her boyfriend, and a family friend were killed in a car accident in August 2005. Only her mother and sister survived.[12] On December 18, 2005, Jenna Johnson, Jessica's teammate, died of a heart defect while she was training to run in a charity marathon.[13] She was twenty-two and worked as a production assistant on *The George Lopez Show*. George and Ann Lopez felt they had lost a family member when

Jenna died. The Lopez family paid for all of her funeral expenses.[14]

A happy memento was located in the kitchen between the door and the stairs. That is where George Lopez's Caddyshack Award sat. He vowed that it would be there as long as the show was on the air. He received the award at the California Golf Writers Banquet. "It was so funny the night I received the award," he said, "because everyone was getting Waterford crystal and I got this trophy that looks like you bought it on your way out of Tijuana with some gum."[15]

The California Golf Writers Association gives the award to honor a famous person (an actor, comic, musician, etc.) who makes positive contributions to golf. The name *Caddyshack* came from the 1980 Bill Murray movie, a comedy about a golf course with a gopher problem. In fact, Bill Murray received the first Caddyshack Award. Other winners include musician Huey Lewis and actors Kevin Costner and William Devane.[16]

Inside his dressing room, George Lopez had shrines to Freddie Prinze and the other great comedian who influenced him—Richard Pryor. A picture of Freddie hung on the wall. Richard Pryor's 1984 Nikes rest in a protective case. "Richard" is on the back of one heel while "Pryor" is on the other one. There is also a card from Pryor's widow that reads: "George Lopez, so you can follow in Richard's footsteps."

A lot has changed since 1974 when Chico Rodriguez (Freddie Prinze) rode his bicycle into Ed Brown's garage on *Chico and the Man*. As of 2007, there were approximately 41.3 million Latinos in the United States. They are the largest ethnic minority. Spanish is so widespread that some call it the second language of the United States. Latino cooking has become so popular that salsa has replaced ketchup as the number one condiment. For a long time, Latinos have played Major League Baseball. No longer are Latinos just baseball stars. Now they own and manage major league teams. They are also politicians, singers, actors, and much more.[17]

George Lopez said: "Very evident to me, and I think others, is the job that Latinos do in the United States, whether it's cooking, cleaning, gardening. We're doctors and lawyers and politicians and really everything."[18]

He had tapped into a growing market. Latinos represent $700 billion a year in buying power and 11.2 million homes with TV sets. He was very pleased that ninety percent of the audience for *The George Lopez Show* was not Latino.[19] If only Latinos watched, he would not be able to cross cultures and promote understanding. Without viewers of all colors and all ethnic backgrounds, *The George Lopez Show* would not have had a season premiere that made it the top show in its time slot. A large part of the show's success was due to scripts that appealed to a wide range of viewers.

Lopez's stand-up comedy routine appealed to millions as well. When he first got started in the business, he often played to half-empty rooms. Now, all his shows sell out. There is standing room only, no matter where he goes. He has shattered the myth that only Latinos will come to hear a Latino comedian. He also shatters attendance records from coast to coast. In October 2003, he became one of the few comedians to sell out Los Angeles' historic Universal Amphitheater for three straight nights (October 10–12). A year later, in December 2004, he set an attendance record at the same place. More than forty-two thousand people went to his seven-night performances. Every night was sold-out.

Playing off the popularity of singer and actress Jennifer Lopez (J. Lo), George Lopez calls himself "G. Lo, the *other* Lopez" or "the Lopez you're not sick of."[20]

At the end of each television season, George Lopez did not head to the beach to soak up the sunshine and rest and relax. Instead, he went on the road with his stand-up comedy act because he liked to connect with people. He called it "Summer Fun."[21] Although he has been in movies and has made lots of television appearances, doing stand-up comedy is the work he loves best.

George Lopez loves to hear people laugh. On television, he knew he made millions of people laugh, but it was a different experience. He could only hear the people in the studio react to his comedy. On a concert tour, he soaks up the energy of the live audience.[22]

Some of his comedy routines contain words that might offend certain audiences. He tailors his language to fit the situation. Once, when he was in San Antonio, Texas, he peeped out before a performance to see what kind of audience had shown up. He said it looked like "ten A.M. at First Baptist Church."[23] He made a split-second decision to take out the four-letter words, eliminate situations that might offend the crowd, and change the routine. It worked! The crowd loved it.[24]

Onstage, George Lopez does not use many props. Usually, he only needs a microphone, a microphone stand, a table for towels, water bottles, and a high-backed chair. His style of comedy is very physical and tiring. He paces around the stage, dashes from left to

George Lopez performs his stand-up comedy at the Don Haskins Center in El Paso, Texas, on June 23, 2007.

Snippets from George Lopez's Comedy Routine

His neighborhood (Pebble Beach, a private community near Monterey.): "I live in a very white neighborhood and sometimes I make chorizo just for the smell, just to get it in the air . . . I don't know what they thought would happen when I moved in. I'm very quiet. None of us have roosters any more. My car starts the first time."[26]

On relationships: "We never try to do anything professionally. All my aunts would dye their hair in the front yard on Saturday mornings. Even if they wanted to go to a beauty salon, my grandmother wouldn't let them."

"Adónde vas, Janet?"

"I'm going to go get my hair done."

"*Mira*, Miss Clairol. Get over here . . . Get it nice and lovely. *Siéntate* . . . It's a sunny day. We'll do it in the front yard. *Mira*. Get the hose and wet your hair while I go get a towel and a clothes pin."[27]

Everyday life: "One thing Mexicans never do is look at the . . . owner's manual . . . Mexicans don't use the manual because we have a Manuel. 'Hey, Manuel! My car . . .'"[28]

His family: (On a trip to Disneyland when he asked his grandmother for a Mickey Mouse hat, the kind with ears and his name embroidered across the front): "One, you're lucky we brought you. Two, you want a souvenir, save your ticket. Three, your ears stick out more than the hat. Here, I'll just write your name across your forehead."[29]

Attitudes toward work: "Mexicans are always late. You want to trip someone up? Be early."[30]

Medicine: "Latino people, we never go to the doctor. We could be coughing blood, and still we won't go."[31]

Love: "The Chicano 'I love you' is: 'I'm here, ain't I? Where am I going? Where am I going? All my tools are at your mom's house. I ain't going.'"[32]

On Anglos: "I'm a huge fan of reality shows. I mean, I thought the first one—*Dukes of Hazzard*—captured white people perfectly."[33]

right, crouches down, jumps up, and sometimes falls down on purpose. The microphone stand becomes a lamp, a kid, his dance partner—almost anything. After a performance, he is so tired, he feels like he has gone ten rounds with boxing great Oscar De La Hoya.[34]

Most of his comedy routines come from people, places, and things in his past. Sometimes, he uses current events. Sometimes, he bases it on his life right now.

During breaks from his television show and stand-up comedy, George Lopez visits other television shows. He has appeared on more than one hundred, including *The Tonight Show with Jay Leno*, Showtime's *Latino Laugh Festival*, and ABC's *Politically Incorrect with Bill Maher*. Before he got his own show, he was a frequent host on *¡Qué Locos!*, a comedy show on a Spanish network. He also had recurring roles on the Nickelodeon series *The Brothers Garcia* and Showtime's *Resurrection Boulevard*.

He also worked on movies when not filming *The George Lopez Show*. In 2004, he starred in an ABC-TV movie *Naughty or Nice*. He played a shock jock (a controversial radio disc jockey) who learns that Christmas miracles can happen. His wife, Ann Lopez, produced the movie.[35]

The same year, he wrote the story of his life. An award-winning writer, Armen Keteyian co-authored *Why You Crying?* It became a best-seller on the *New York Times* list.

In the 2005 children's movie *The Adventures of Shark Boy and Lava Girl in 3-D*, George Lopez had the role of

George Lopez holds his new autobiography *Why You Crying?* at a book-signing at Barnes & Noble in New York on May 25, 2004. The book was co-written with Emmy Award winning writer and sportscaster Armen Keteyian.

both the good guy and the bad guy. The movie tells the story of Max, a lonely ten-year-old boy who has two imaginary friends, Shark Boy and Lava Girl. Shark Boy is half-boy, half-shark and was raised by great white sharks. Lava Girl has flaming hair and shoots flames and lava rocks from her hands. She melts everything she touches.

No one believes Shark Boy and Lava Girl exist until they show up one day in Max's class. The teacher, Mr. Electricidad (George Lopez), becomes an instant believer when Shark Boy and Lava Girl crash through his classroom wall one day looking for Max. The villain, Mr. Electric (also played by George Lopez), threatens to destroy their home planet, and they need Max's help to stop him. Mr. Electric, who looks like a giant alarm clock with electric currents for arms and legs, plans to cast a spell that will keep children from sleeping.[36] That will destroy all their dreams.

The movie is shot in 3-D, a special three-dimensional filming process. To see the movie in 3-D and to get the full effect, the audience has to watch it using cardboard glasses with red and green filters.[37] The real world in the movie is shown in 2-D, but all dream and fantasy scenes are in 3-D.[38]

George Lopez enjoys making movies, but his first love will always be stand-up comedy. Over the years, he has recorded a number of comedy CDs and DVDs (*Right Now Right Now, El Más Chingón,* and *Why You Crying?*) that have done very well. One of them, *Team Leader,* was nominated for the "Best Comedy Album" Grammy in 2004, up against albums by Garrison Keillor, "Weird Al" Yankovic, Margaret Cho, and David Cross.[39] George Lopez recorded the CD at the Ice House in Pasadena between taping episodes of *The George Lopez Show*.

His popularity grew and grew. Between December 8 and December 14, 2005, the Harris Poll asked 960 U.S. adults: Who is your favorite TV personality? Oprah Winfrey was America's favorite for the fourth year in a row. George Lopez made the list for the first time and came in at Number 9.[40]

Forbes magazine named him to its 2006 "Celebrity 100" list. The year before, Lopez made $12 million. Over $8 million of his income came from doing stand-up comedy. Wherever he went, his show sold out. In the August 22, 2005, edition of *Time* magazine, George Lopez was named one of the twenty-five most influential Hispanics in America.[41]

Because of his popularity, several interesting guest stars dropped by *The George Lopez Show*. Visitors included sports figures (Rod Carew, Steve Garvey, Joe Morgan, Jim Palmer, Laila Ali, Donovan McNabb), William Hung from *American Idol*, the movie director Robert Rodriguez (*Shark Boy and Lava Girl in 3-D*), and actresses Eva Longoria (*Desperate Housewives*) and Hillary Duff.

Politicians have visited, too. Antonio Villaraigosa, the mayor of Los Angeles, played himself. Rita Moreno, an actress from Puerto Rico, played Benny's mother

George Lopez, left, performs with Los Angeles Mayor Antonio Villaraigosa on the set of *The George Lopez Show*, on September I, 2005, in Burbank, California. Lopez pushed to get Villaraigosa on his ABC series.

(George Lopez's grandmother).[42] She is one of the only actresses to have won an Emmy, an Oscar, a Tony, and a Grammy Award.

George Lopez had a special connection to one of his guests—Freddie Prinze, Jr.[43] He had watched his father's television show and had been inspired by it. He was now in a position to help his idol's son.

A Hole-in-One
for George

"Free churros for everyone!"[1]

      —George Lopez as the new host of the Bob Hope
      Chrysler Classic

On March 7, 2004, George Lopez bounced onto the stage of the TV Land Awards ceremony and danced about for a bit to the tune "Lowrider." He was very excited and proud because he was about to present an award honoring his idol, Freddie Prinze, Sr.

"In 1974," George Lopez said, "mainstream television ventured into the *barrio* for the first time with a situation comedy that recognized the growing importance and relevance of Latino culture . . . That show was called *Chico and the Man* . . . It was a very important step forward and tonight we honor *Chico and the Man* with the TV Land Visionary Award and it is truly an honor I

never thought I would have and I truly am touched . . .
I love you, Freddie."[2]

A young man got up to accept the award. He slowly
climbed the steps to the stage. He was very emotional
because he was going to accept the award for his father.
The young man was Freddie Prinze, Jr. He gave George
Lopez a big hug and whispered "Stay here with me."[3]

George Lopez did just that. It was the first time
Prinze, Jr., had acknowledged his dad in public. He was
only ten months old when his father died. There had
always been a cloud over his death. Some said that
Freddie, Sr., shot himself accidentally. Others said it was
suicide. Because of the questions about his father's
death, parents sometimes would not let Freddie, Jr.,
play with their children. He heard people say bad things
about his dad.

When Freddie Prinze, Jr., grew up in Arizona, he did
not know there was a Mexican-American teenager in
California who loved *Chico and the Man*. He did not
know that the teenager would become a famous
comedian who would help Prinze, Jr., restore his
father's good name.[4]

Now, as Prinze, Jr., accepted the award from George
Lopez, he said: "I am proud of what my father accomplished in such a short period of time . . . and
it makes my heart soar when I see other people share
that pride."[5]

Another proud moment came when Freddie Prinze,
Sr., got a star on the Hollywood Walk of Fame, a

sidewalk that runs along Hollywood Boulevard and Vine Street in Los Angeles, California.[6]

The Walk of Fame honors anyone who has made an important contribution to the entertainment industry (radio, television, motion pictures, recording, live performance).[7] Many people have received stars, including magician Harry Houdini, actress Rita Moreno, author Dr. Seuss, and cartoonist Walt Disney. Fictional characters have stars too: Godzilla, Bugs Bunny, Mickey Mouse. Even dogs, such as Lassie, can have stars.

After George Lopez got his TV show in 2002, he moved to a new house and learned that Kathy Prinze, Freddie Prinze's widow, lived four doors down. They

From the right, Freddie Prinze, Jr.; his mother, Kathy Cochran; and George Lopez attend Freddie Prinze, Sr.'s Hollywood Walk of Fame Star Ceremony on Hollywood Boulevard on December 14, 2004.

became friends. Then, one day, Kathy gave George Lopez a key chain and an old American Express card that had once belonged to her husband. A little later, he met her son.

George Lopez thought Freddie Prinze, Sr., deserved a star on the Hollywood Walk of Fame and he worked hard to make it happen. The star was unveiled in December 2004, twenty years after the premiere of *Chico and the Man*. George Lopez also helped Freddie Prinze, Jr., get a deal with ABC for a sitcom.

Freddie Prinze, Jr., was grateful for all of George Lopez's help. Prinze, Jr., said:

> George Lopez says without Freddie Prinze there's no George Lopez. . . . But without George Lopez, my father never gets his star. Without George Lopez, nobody says good stuff about my father. And the fact that he goes above and beyond to help me, after he's succeeded, that's a big deal to me. I can count on one hand the people who have character who do that in this business. But it's always guys like George Lopez. It's always the people who have been disrespected and who have not been treated well their whole lives who say, "I'm not going to let that happen to some-body else."[8]

The lives and careers of George Lopez and Freddie Prinze, Jr., are connected by the star of *Chico and the Man*. His tragic death affected both of them deeply. In 2005–2006, they were linked in another way with back-to-back sitcoms on ABC. For the first time ever, there were two shows about Latino families.

The George Lopez Show tells the story of a working-class Mexican-American family in Los Angeles. In *Freddie*, the family is Puerto Rican and lives in Chicago. Freddie Prinze, Jr., plays a chef who owns an upscale restaurant while George Lopez is the plant manager of an airplane company.[9] In *The George Lopez Show*, the main characters speak English. Occasionally there is a word in Spanish. *Freddie* is different. The actress who plays the grandmother only speaks Spanish. English subtitles tell the viewer what she is saying.

> **"Don't watch because we are a couple of Latino guys."**

When Freddie Prinze, Jr., got a show after George Lopez's, people started calling it "the Latino Hour." George Lopez did not like that. He wanted people to watch the shows because they thought they were funny. "Don't watch because we are a couple of Latino guys," George Lopez said. "Shows should just be . . . shows without hyphenating their lead characters."[10]

Freddie did not last long. It started on October 12, 2005, but was cancelled the next spring. The final episode aired on May 31, 2006.

On March 29, 2006, George Lopez was honored with a star on the Hollywood Walk of Fame. His is located near the ones for Queen Latifah, Winnie the Pooh, and Sandra Bullock. It is the 2306th Star on the Walk of Fame and is located at 6801 Hollywood Boulevard. It

George Lopez points to his star on the Hollywood Walk of Fame during dedication ceremonies in Los Angeles on March 29, 2006.

celebrates the one hundredth episode of *The George Lopez Show*, a major milestone for a television series.[11] It is the first time a show about a Latino family has reached that landmark.[12]

Attending the ceremony were George Lopez's wife and daughter, Ann and Mayan Lopez, the mayor of Los Angeles, Antonio Villaraigosa, and other important people.

"My grandparents told me I'd end up on the street," Lopez joked. "And I did—the Hollywood Walk of Fame."[13]

He ended up on the golf course as well. On December 24, 2006, the Professional Golfer's Association of America (PGA) asked him to host the 2007 Bob Hope Chrysler Classic. The PGA is dedicated to promoting the game of golf and maintaining professional standards. It conducts more than thirty tournaments.[14]

George Lopez was on the set of his show at Warner Brothers Studios in Burbank, California, when the announcement was made. A big grin spread across his face. His dimples popped out. He was excited and happy to be the new host. George Lopez was in charge of the only event on the 2007 PGA tour with a celebrity host.[15]

The tournament sponsor, the Chrysler car company, gave George Lopez a limited production high performance black 2007 300C SRT8 Chrysler. George Lopez was glad to get the car, but he felt even happier to be the

George Lopez smiles as he looks skyward during the celebrity challenge of the AT&T Pebble Beach National Pro-Am golf tournament on February 8, 2006, at the Pebble Beach golf links in Pebble Beach, California. Lopez has a house near the golf course.

host of the best celebrity pro-am event on the PGA Tour. Pro-am stands for "professional-amateur." During the tournament, professionals who golf for a living play with amateurs who do it only for fun and because they love the sport. The Bob Hope Chrysler Classic is the only golf tournament played on four courses over five days. It took place from January 15–21, 2007.[16] Celebrities and athletes played with professional golfers. It started in Palm Springs on January 15 and moved on to Pebble Beach.

> **"(I'm) not a better golfer, but I think a better person."**

George Lopez loves golf: "It's helped me with my life, my life skills and you know, [I'm] not a better golfer, but I think a better person."[17]

For the twelve-year-old boy who learned golf by hitting lemons in his backyard, hosting the PGA Tour was a dream come true. Now that George Lopez is a successful stand-up comic who had a popular sitcom, he can feed his golfing passion. He has a house at Pebble Beach, home to one of the best golf courses in the world. He is a member at Lakeside Golf Club in Burbank, California, where Bob Hope played.

The five-day event was called the "Bob Hope Chrysler Classic hosted by George Lopez."[18] Hope began the tournament in 1960. Over the years, it has raised millions of dollars for charity. Bob Hope, a comedian and movie star, got important Hollywood stars to participate.[19] Bing Crosby, Dean Martin, Sammy Davis, Jr., and others were happy to help out. Not only did they play golf, they joked with the people who had come to watch them play.

By the 1990s, Bob Hope was in his nineties and in bad health. The Bob Hope Chrysler Classic began to fade. Then, at age 100, Bob Hope died.

George Lopez wanted to bring some sparkle back to the event.[20] For his first year as host, he drew some big names: movie stars (Clint Eastwood, Samuel L. Jackson, Andy Garcia, Don Cheadle, Huey Lewis, Joe Pesci, Cheech Marin), sports figures (Roger Clemens, Marcus Allen, Oscar De La Hoya, Sterling Sharpe), and television stars (Jimmy Kimmel).

George Lopez did it! Officials in charge of the PGA tournament declared it the most successful one in its seventy-year history. The Pro-Am raised $5.84 million for local charities.[21]

Lopez not only hosted the golf tournament. He played too. He got to do what he likes best: golf, hang around with his friends, and joke around with his fans. Whenever he golfs, he especially likes to reach across the ropes that separate the players from the spectators and shake people's hands. Sometimes he gives kids his hat and glove.[22] Lopez clowns around while the crowd cheers on his antics. He waves, shouts, gestures with his golf club, dances around, does the splits, and pretends to be riding a skateboard.[23]

George Lopez wants to make the tournament fun for people to come and watch, even if he is the butt of the joke. Once, when he hit a shot far into the woods, the sports commentator said: "That ball is so far into the wood, if it was wrapped in bacon, Lassie wouldn't even find it." George Lopez thought it was a brilliant, funny comment.[24] As Lopez always says, "If we can't laugh at ourselves and others, who's left?"[25]

George Lopez is very proud of his Mexican heritage and even has little Mexican flags sewn on the leather covers of his golf clubs. He wants to change the way people think about Latinos, and he thinks that golf might do that. His audiences, he likes to point out, are made up of white and brown, young and old. "We [Chicanos] just try to be people, general regular people. Except we've got great tans," he once quipped.[26]

George Lopez was asked to host the 2008 Bob Hope Chrysler Classic as well. He wants to make the tournament the hottest stop on the PGA Tour.[27]

Whether it was his television show, his comedy routine, or his golf game, George Lopez likes to connect with people everywhere. He said he is "a Mexican Mickey Mouse."[28]

He also likes to drive the car Chrysler gave him when he became the tournament host. "That thing goes fast," he remarked. "As you know, Latinos are not used to going fast, so I like it. I've gotten it up to, you know, 55."[29]

What does George Lopez do when he's not traveling from comedy club to comedy club or playing golf?

He works tirelessly to promote his favorite causes. He and his wife are involved in a number of charity events. One of his favorites is First Tee. He feels he has learned a lot from the game of golf and it has made him a better person. He wants youngsters to have the same experience. That is why he supports First Tee, a junior golf program that introduces inner-city youth to golf. It also teaches values such as honesty, integrity, sportsmanship, respect, courtesy, judgment, confidence, responsibility, and perseverance.[30]

George and Ann Lopez continue to work in "The George Lopez & Ann Lopez-Richie Alarcón CARE Foundation" that they set up in 2001 with Richard Alarcón, a state senator from California. It was named in memory of Alarcón's young son Richie who died in a traffic accident in 1987. The purpose of the foundation is to support community arts and education. It has bought a truck for a food bank that helps thirty-thousand people a month, given aid to the Latino Theatre Company, and sponsored leadership training for the Young Senators Program. The foundation's good work helps the entire community.[31]

George Lopez is on the board of the Starlight Starbright Children's Foundation, a charity that helps terminally ill children and their families. Its mission is to brighten the lives of seriously ill children. He also raises money for it.[32]

George and Ann Lopez arrive at the National Kidney Foundation's 28th Annual Gift of Life Celebration on April 29, 2007, in Burbank, California. The two are spokespeople for the foundation.

Another cause that is dear to him is "We Care for Youth," an organization that helps young people develop job skills. Based in Los Angeles, it focuses on at-risk teenagers and tries to improve their lives.[33]

George Lopez got involved with one charity completely against his wishes: The National Kidney Foundation. He said:

> When I got sick, I went to the doctor and I said to him, "Look, I don't want to be the poster boy for kidney disease. I just want to get this done and resume my life." . . . But then, when I woke up two days after my surgery, I felt better than I ever have in my life and I saw people who were sick and I said, "I can't turn my back on them."[34]

Now George and Ann Lopez are spokespeople for the National Kidney Foundation and are very active in their local chapter of the National Kidney Foundation.[35] George Lopez has completely recovered from his kidney transplant. Along with Ann Lopez, he works tirelessly to promote organ donation.

The Lopezes wear lime-green bracelets to remind people to donate organs and save lives. Ann Lopez likes to tell her story so that people will not be afraid to be a live donor. They serve as Honorary Chairs of the National Kidney Foundation's Kidney Walk Program, a series of 5K walks held throughout the United States to promote kidney health awareness.

In June 2006, George and Ann Lopez participated in the U.S. Transplant Games, an Olympic-style event for recipients of every type of lifesaving organ transplant. It was held in Louisville, Kentucky. Ann Lopez spoke at the Opening Ceremonies and was the keynote speaker at the Donor Recognition Ceremony. More than two thousand athletes who have received transplants of kidney, liver, heart, lung, pancreas, and bone marrow competed for gold, silver, and bronze medals. There were dozens of events, including track and field, swimming, cycling, racquetball, and basketball.[36]

Sure enough, George Lopez did what he loved best. He golfed as part of the team from Southern California.[37] All the athletes played their best and showed that having a transplant did not slow them down or change their ability to do what they enjoyed.

> "Sandra Bullock has been great to me from day one."

Sandra Bullock said, "The love and respect I have for Ann and George Lopez has doubled knowing how they have struggled with this [kidney disease] quietly for the past several years."[38]

For their part, the Lopez family admires Bullock for taking a risk with the television show. As George Lopez once said, "The TV show is going well. . . . And that's really, ultimately, what I wanted to achieve when I started doing standup. Sandra Bullock has been great to me from day one . . . She's just been fantastic and offered every service to us . . . she didn't offer a kidney, but other than that . . ."

Ann Lopez jumped to Sandra Bullock's defense: "She didn't know. She probably would have."[39]

When asked about his health, George Lopez says: "I feel great, I get checked every three months to see how everything is holding up, and I know I may not look like it, but I am in amazing health. I take my medicine everyday . . . That medicine only works if you take it."[40]

George Lopez promotes organ donation, but another concern for him is childhood obesity. The number of overweight or obese children in the United States has doubled in the last twenty years.[41] That can lead to serious health problems. Many medical experts consider it one of the major health care issues in the United States.

George Lopez and Julia Louis-Dreyfus (Elaine on the sitcom *Seinfeld* and Christine on the sitcom *The New Adventures of Old Christine*) made a video entitled "Food and Fitness Matter: Raising Healthy, Active Kids." The video helps parents and schools understand the dangers of childhood obesity. It also gives them information about food and physical fitness for babies, children, and teenagers.

The Spanish version, hosted by George Lopez, gives Latino parents important information and suggestions for healthy living. Julia Louis-Dreyfus hosts the English version.[42] George Lopez says: "I think we Latinos have to be stricter in our diet . . . sometimes we eat food that isn't good for us but it is so tasty!"[43]

George Lopez also likes to promote literacy. In 2006,

he became an official spokesman for the American Library Association (ALA) and hundreds of libraries across the country. He has a library card from the Los Angeles Public Library and encourages everyone to get one. "From homework help to book clubs," he says, "libraries are where it's at. Your library card is your ticket to a world of opportunities. Get it, and use it at your library."[44]

A little later, George Lopez performed in "Comic Relief 2006" on HBO. The show was live at Caesar's Palace in Las Vegas. For twenty years, comedians have been performing on "Comic Relief" TV specials. The money raised on the show goes to charity. In 2006, two hundred fifty thousand dollars went to the victims of Hurricane Katrina and to the city of New Orleans to help it rebuild.

For a man who makes a living at comedy, George Lopez takes charity very seriously.

What's Next?

"If we can't laugh at ourselves and others, who's left?"[1]
—George Lopez

Not everything in George Lopez's life is as serious as his charity work. He likes to tell jokes, but he can be the butt of a joke, too. Recently, on his birthday, George Lopez and his wife came home to a big surprise. Construction workers from the city were about to tear down the wall to his house. They said it was over a sewer main. The wall had to be torn down because that part of his house had been built without a permit.

George Lopez could not understand what was going on. He stayed calm and tried to reason with them. They told him they had sent him five letters warning him that something was wrong with his house. He said he never got the letters.

Ann Lopez put a hard hat on and studied the thick file of paperwork the city had on their house. She acted like she was trying to figure out the problem.

George Lopez was very confused. He did not know what to do.

Then friends came running up to him, jumping and yelling "Happy Birthday!"

At that moment, he realized he had gotten punked. Constance Marie and Ann Lopez had set him up. They were in on the prank.

He was on the television show *Punk'd* on MTV. He looked at his friends and said, "You ought to be ashamed of yourselves . . . Giving an old Chicano a heart attack! . . . I got punked, man! I got punked!"[2]

Another time, George Lopez had something funny happen to him when he needed a new roof. He hired a man to fix the roof:

> [That man in turn hired] fifteen dudes from Mexico . . . There's all this music and they're all up on the roof, and I don't even know how they got on the roof. There's no ladder . . .

> So I come home early one day because it's about 110 in the shade, and I figure I'll go check on them, make sure nobody's stuck to the shingles. Only there's nobody on the roof. "Ah . . . maybe the rope broke and they all fell." So I go in the backyard and I look. Nobody.

> I go to the courtyard. Nobody.

> Finally, I work my way about to the pool, and there they are, all fifteen of them, having a gay old time, drinking Dos Equis, swimming in their *calzones*. Drinking and carrying on, and I'm just waiting and watching in the doorway.

> And one guy looks at me and goes, "Hey, *vato*, jump in, the man's not home."

George Lopez once remarked, "As a Chicano, I never thought that I would live in a house that the Olsen twins once lived in. Maybe I'd work on their house or put in a pool, but to live in it? Wow!"

Apparently, the men he hired to work on his roof were just as surprised. They did not expect a house that grand to be owned by a Chicano.[3]

Ping-pong was the focus of George Lopez's next movie, a comedy called *Balls of Fury*. It premiered in January 2007 and told the story of secret win-or-die ping-pong tournaments. "In the criminal underworld," the movie trailer says, "there is a deadly tournament of champions. Many enter, but only one survives." When an opponent loses a game, he is killed. In one scene, a ping-pong player looks on, distressed, as someone dies. "You killed him," he says in horror.

> "As a Chicano, I never thought that I would live in a house that the Olsen twins once lived in."

"What part of *sudden death* didn't you understand?" the character played by Christopher Walken asks.

George Lopez plays an FBI agent named Ernie Rodriguez who recruits a professional ping-pong player for a secret mission.[4]

The ping-pong player agrees to the mission because he is determined to bounce back and win, but more importantly, he wants to find his father's killer.[5]

On February 24, 2007, George Lopez's one-man comedy special aired on HBO. It was an hour long and was called "George Lopez: America's Mexican." It was the first time he performed all by himself on HBO. For a comedian, HBO is the best TV station to do a comedy show. George Lopez can do or say whatever he wants there because it is cable TV and not network TV.[6] Cable TV does not have as many rules as network TV. "I've already made it," he says, "so I'm not really trying to impress anybody."

The special was filmed live at the Dodge Theater in Phoenix, Arizona. He called the show "Star, Spanglish, Banter" because he was going to talk about a lot of issues that are important to America. Immigration, his family, modern-day kids, old-school values, hybrid cars, cars that run on corn, mental illness, and the future.[7]

He wanted to talk about immigrants because it is a sore spot for many people. "Immigrant labor runs the country," he said in an interview, "and no one has said that and made it funny."[8] He does not mind if the show upsets people. "Con este especial no busco hacer amigos, lo que quiero es crear un debate." ("With this special, I'm not looking to make friends. What I want is to create a debate.")[9]

When asked about racism, he said:

[It] doesn't happen to me, but I know it still happens. I have been confused for a lot of different things: valets or workers. But it never really bothered me. I made fun of it . . . And racism isn't really a proper term. Ignorance is more the term we should use.

Stupidity goes along all colors . . . Stupidity is assumption, and I think there's too much assumption in this country by the way people look. I don't think that's racist, I just think that's ignorance.[10]

He made a special appearance in *Where's Marty?*, a movie filmed completely in Monterey County, California, where he lives. The film raised funds for the Monterey Film Commission and its scholarship program.

George Lopez plays a police officer in *Tortilla Heaven* (2007), a comedy about a small New Mexico town. When the owner of a Mexican restaurant sees the face of Jesus in a tortilla, the town is never the same again.

George Lopez's sense of humor helped him through a dark moment in 2007. On May 15, the network cancelled *The George Lopez Show*. Six seasons is a very long run for a television series.[11] Still, it was a hard blow for the man *People en Español* put on its list of "One Hundred Most Influential Hispanics" in 2007.[12]

At first, he was bitter about the end of his show. "I get kicked out for a . . . caveman . . . So a Chicano can't be on TV, but a caveman can?" The television series *Cavemen* is based on car insurance commercials with actors playing cavemen. The show premiered on October 2, 2007, on ABC.

Later, George Lopez said: "I'll take the good and the bad. My popularity, I was involved in charities, I overcame my illness, all on TV. I shared all of that with America, every secret I had."[13]

George Lopez and Constance Marie, playing concerned parents, talk to their son, played by Luis Armand Garcia. *The George Lopez Show* was cancelled on May 15, 2007.

Cancellation by ABC was not really the end of the show. On September 17, 2007, *The George Lopez Show* went into syndication. That means that the profits from the television show will soar. Syndication is important in television. *Friends* made about one billion dollars when it went into syndication. *Who's the Boss* (Tony Danza's sitcom) took in $600 million.

George Lopez's show was making a lot of money for ABC, but everyone knew the big money would come if it went into syndication. The ABC network had bought the rights to broadcast the show once a week. Syndication meant that the program will be sold to television stations and cable channels all across the United States. It will be shown in different time slots. Some stations even show it five days a week.[14]

In 2007, George Lopez earned $5 million from his show's final season; $9 million from one year of stand-up comedy shows; and $15 million from the syndication deal.

"I am the living example of the American dream,"

Filmography

George Lopez acted in the following movies:

Ski Patrol (1990)
Fatal Instinct (1993)
Bread and Roses (2001)
Real Women Have Curves (2002)
Naughty or Nice (2004)
The Adventures of Shark Boy and Lava Girl in 3-D (2005)
Where's Marty? (2006)
Balls of Fury (2007)
Tortilla Heaven (2007)
Swing Vote (2008)
South of the Border (2008)
Henry Poole is Here (2008)
The Richest Man in the World (2008)

he said. "I came from no place. No place! No father. No mother. Nobody in the family who believed in me. And this year [2007], my show went into syndication which means George Lopez ain't going nowhere!"[15]

The George Lopez Show will live on in reruns in the same way that Desi Arnaz's *I Love Lucy* from the 1950s lives on.

Although the show is over, George Lopez still works in movies and stand-up comedy.

George Lopez has roles in four films coming out in 2008. In *The Richest Man in the World,* he plays a poor man who gets to live in the world of the richest man alive. *Henry Poole is Here* and *Swing Vote* also debut in 2008. George Lopez is the voice of Papi, a male chihuahua in *South of the Border*, a live-action talking animal picture about a chihuahua lost in Mexico.

George Lopez has done it all. His autobiography, *Why You Crying?* (2004), was on the *New York Times* Bestsellers Top Twenty. He has made award-winning movies, like *Bread and Roses*. His comedy CDs have earned him Grammy nominations. When he performs in concert, he sells out from coast to coast.

The George Lopez Show made George Lopez one of the best-known Latinos on television. Success brought him money, houses in California and Hawaii, fancy cars, a star on Hollywood's Walk of Fame, and other perks.[16] George Lopez says: "If I was into thieving, I'd be the first dude I'd rob."[17]

Lopez performs at the 35th Annual Just for Laughs Festival on July 20, 2007, in Montreal, Canada.

Although he has worked in every field in entertainment, George Lopez thinks of himself as a stand-up comedian. He maintains a very active schedule and has sold out most of the top comedy clubs in the United States.[18] He recently did a stand-up comedy show at Gibson Amphitheater in Universal City, California. It sold out, too. Fifty thousand tickets sold for eight nights is a terrific success.[19] Sometimes George Lopez returns to his old haunts. He likes to drop by the Ice House Comedy Club to test new material. The audience is always surprised and delighted to see him walk on stage.[20]

> **"I don't have to apologize for being successful."**

When asked about success, George Lopez peers into the front rows of his audience and points. "That's how you know you've made it: when you've got a whole row of güeros [fair-skinned persons]."[21]

Successful Latinos often feel they have to downplay their accomplishments because friends and family will get jealous.[22] Not George Lopez:

I don't have to apologize for being successful. I don't have to apologize for having a house in Hawaii. I don't have to apologize for anything. . . . Would Donald Trump apologize if he bought a yacht? He'd show it off. Us, we'd probably have it dry-docked somewhere, saying "Don't tell my tia [aunt] I bought a boat because I owe her $75." That's the way we are.[23]

So what's next for George Lopez? He has a lot of projects in the works. But no matter how busy or successful he gets, he will always have time for golf. George Lopez was overjoyed when he played in his first AT&T golf tournament. In his group, he had one Anglo and Andy Garcia. "Andy and I are the first two Latinos to play together here," George Lopez joked. "They were going to put [another Latino] in our group, but three Latinos is a gang."[24]

Ann Lopez sums up her husband's accomplishments this way: "I am so proud of George Lopez. I am in awe of all that he has accomplished as a man, as a husband, as a father, and as a performer."[25]

George Lopez said it best on a video segment for the TV Guide channel called *Sixty Seconds Life Story:* "I have managed to turn tragic events into comedy. And in sixty seconds I can tell you I've never been happier from a place that started sadder. So thank you."[26]

Chronology

April 23, 1961—Born in Mission Hills, California.

September 13, 1974—*Chico and the Man*, George Lopez's favorite show, debuts.

January 29, 1977—Freddie Prinze, star of *Chico and the Man*, dies.

June 4, 1979—Lopez goes on stage for the first time.

August 6, 1979—Lopez graduates from high school.

1979–1987—Works for a number of companies, including an airplane-parts factory.

July 17, 1987—Decides to becomes a full-time comedian; quits his job and goes on the road.

May 1989—Meets Ann Serrano while performing in a comedy club.

September 18, 1993—Marries Ann Serrano.

1996—Daughter, Mayan, born.

2000—Acts in *Bread and Roses*, a movie that wins five awards including one at the Santa Barbara International Film Festival.

2002—Appears in *Real Women Have Curves*, a movie that wins an award at the Sundance Film Festival.

March 27, 2002—*The George Lopez Show* debuts.

March 2003—Performs for President Bush and his wife in Washington, D.C.

2004—Autobiography, *Why You Crying?*, is published.

December 14, 2004—Freddie Prinze gets a star on the Hollywood Walk of Fame.

April 19, 2005—Kidney transplant operation.

2005–2006—George Lopez and Freddie Prinze, Jr., have back-to-back shows on ABC.

2005—Lopez has multiple roles in *The Adventures of Shark Boy and Lava Girl in 3-D*.

March 29, 2006—Gets a star on the Hollywood Walk of Fame.

January 2007—Hosts the Bob Hope Chrysler Classic.

February 2007—Named one of 100 most influential Hispanics by *People en Español*.

February 24, 2007—HBO special, *America's Mexican*.

May 15, 2007—ABC cancels *The George Lopez Show*.

September 17, 2007—*The George Lopez Show* goes into syndication.

Chapter Notes

CHAPTER 1. THE SECRET PATIENT

1. "Ann and George Lopez," *National Kidney Foundation*, 2007, <http://www.kidney.org/patients/George Lopez.cfm> (November 2, 2007).

2. Matt McMillen, "Perfect Match," *WebMD the Magazine*, May/June 2006, <http://www.webmd.com/content/article/121/114100.htm> (November 2, 2007).

3. "Your Kidneys and How They Work," *National Kidney and Urologic Diseases Information Clearinghouse*, NIH Publication No. 06–4241, November 2005, <http://kidney.niddk.nih.gov/kudiseases/pubs/yourkidneys> (Nov. 2, 2007).

4. Sheri and Bob Stritof, "George Lopez and Ann Serano [sic]," *About.com: Marriage*, 2007, <http://marriage.about.com/od/quotes/a/George Lopezann.htm> (November 12, 2007).

5. Interview by Larry King, "Interview with Ann and George Lopez," *CNN.com*, June 9, 2005, <http://edition.cnn.com/TRANSCRIPTS/0506/09/lkl.01.html> (Nov. 2, 2007).

6. Ibid.

7. Ibid.

8. Ibid.

9. Ibid.

10. "Comedian To Help Fight Kidney Disease Since Having A Kidney Transplant," *National Kidney Foundation of Southern California*, October 4, 2005, <www.kidneysocal.org/New_Folder2/George Lopezannpr.doc> (November 11, 2007).

11. Interview with Larry King, "Interview with Ann and George Lopez."

12. "George López recibe un Transplante de Riñón," *People en Español*, February 2007, <http://www.peopleenespanol.com/pespanol/articles/0,22490,1054529,00.html> (November 12, 2007).

13. Stritof.

14. Bella Mahaya Carter, "George and Ann Lopez Share The Gift of Life," Studio City Sun, Vol. 4, No. 7. March 24–30, 2006, <http://suncomm.globat.com/~suncommu/archives/studio_city_sun_archives/2006/March%2024/STU_032406.pdf> (November 11, 2007).

15. Interview with Larry King, "Interview with Ann and George Lopez."

16. Interview with Larry King, "Interview with Ann and George Lopez."

CHAPTER 2. "WHY YOU CRYING?"

1. "George Lopez: The Early Years," *13gb.com Videos*, 2007, <http://13gb.com/media.php?media_id=1193> (November 11, 2007).

2. George Lopez, *Why You Crying?: My Long, Hard Look at Life, Love, and Laughter* (New York: Touchstone Books, 2004), p. 17.

3. Mireya Navarro, "A Life So Sad Had to Be Funny," *New York Times*. November 27, 2007, p. E1.

4. Lopez, p. 184.

5. Ibid., p. 2.

6. Navarro, p. E1.

7. Lopez, pp. 18–20.

8. Ibid., p. 2.

9. Ibid., p. 1.

10. Ibid., p. 17, 34.

11. Interview by Larry King, "Interview with Ann and George Lopez," *CNN.com*, June 9, 2005, <http://edition.cnn.com/TRANSCRIPTS/0506/09/lkl.01.html> (Nov. 2, 2007).
12. Lopez, p. 11.
13. Phillip Rodriguez, "Brown is the New Green: George Lopez and the American Dream," *PBS*, September 12, 2007.
14. George Lopez, "Holmes Depot," *Right Now Right Now.* 2002.
15. "George López, a la Conquista de América," *People en Español*, February 22, 2007, <http://www.peopleenespanol.com/pespanol/articles/0,22490,1592930_2,00.html> (November 12, 2007).
16. Lopez, *Why You Crying?* pp. 8–9.
17. Ibid., p. 34.
18. Ibid., p. 26.
19. Ibid., p. 56.
20. Ibid., p. 26.
21. George Lopez, "George's Stand-up Clips," *Warner Brothers Entertainment, Inc.*, 2004, <http://www2.warnerbros.com/web/George Lopez/moreGeorgeLopez_player.jsp?udk=gl_clip06> (November 12, 2007).
22. Lopez, *Why You Crying?* p. 30.
23. Ibid., p. 28.
24. Ibid., p. 20.
25. Ibid., pp. 20–21.
26. "George Lopez," *Newsmakers*, Issue 4, Gale Group, 2003, <http://www.galeschools.com/hispanic_heritage/bio/lopez_g.htm> (December 8, 2007).
27. Jamie Malanowski, "How Funny People Got that Way," *Readers Digest*, September 2004, <http://www.rd.com/content/famous-comedians-paths-to-stardom/2/> (November 12, 2007).
28. Lopez, *Why You Crying?* p. 23.

CHAPTER 3. A LOVE FOR COMEDY

1. Phillip Rodriguez, "Brown is the New Green: George Lopez and the American Dream," *PBS*, September 12, 2007.

2. "Chico and the Man," AOL Video, 2007, <http://video.aol.com/video-category/chico-and-the-man/1565> (November 10, 2007).

3. "Chico and the Man," *Chico and the Man Online*, 2007, <www.sitcomsonline.com/chicoandtheman.html> (November 10, 2007).

4. George Lopez, *Why You Crying?: My Long, Hard Look at Life, Love, and Laughter* (New York: Touchstone Books, 2004), p. 41.

5. Eric Deggans, "Freddie Prinze, Jr.: Taking Back His Father's Name," *Hispanic Magazine.com*, September 2005, <http://www.hispaniconline.com/magazine/2005/September/Cover Story/> (November 4, 2007).

6. "Chico and the Man," *Chico and the Man Online*.

7. Ibid.

8. Ibid.

9. Jamie Malanowski, "How Funny People Got that Way," *Reader's Digest*, September 2004, <http://www.rd.com/content/famous-comedians-paths-to-stardom/2/> (November 12, 2007).

10. "George López, a la Conquista de América," *People en Español*, February 22, 2007, <http://www.peopleenespanol.com/pespanol/articles/0,22490,1592930_2,00.html> (November 12, 2007).

11. Lopez, p. 65.

12. Ibid., p. 55.

13. Ibid., p. 67.14. Vilma Maldonado, "Latino Comedian to Perform His First Valley Show," December 28, 2001, <http://www.georgelopez.com/news/01_05.html> (November 12, 2007).

15. Gerry Gittelson, "Comedian Lopez Proves He's a Survivor," *Daily News*, November 12, 2001, <http://www.george lopez.com/news/01_06.html> (November 12, 2007).

16. "George Lopez," *Newsmakers*, Issue 4, Gale Group, 2003.

17. "The Ice House History," 2007, <http://www.icehouse comedy.com/html/history.htm> (November 4, 2007).

18. "Seeing Stars: Live On Stage," *The Ice House*, 2007, <http://www.seeing-stars.com/OnStage/IceHouse. shtml> (November 4, 2007).

19. Lopez, pp. 78–79.

CHAPTER 4. GEORGE AND ANN LOPEZ

1. Interview by Larry King, "Interview with Ann and George Lopez," *CNN.com*, June 9, 2005, <http://edition.cnn.com/ TRANSCRIPTS/0506/09/lkl.01.html> (Nov. 2, 2007).

2. George Lopez, *Why You Crying?: My Long, Hard Look at Life, Love, and Laughter* (New York: Touchstone Books, 2004), pp. 78–91.

3. Ibid., pp. 79–80.

4. Ibid., p. 83.

5. Sheri and Bob Stritof, "George and Ann Lopez," 2007, <http://marriage.about.com/od/entertainmen1/p/George Lopez.htm> (November 4, 2007).

6. *"Gift of Life from a Comedian's Wife,"* ABC News Primetime Live, May 12, 2005.

7. Lopez, p. 191.

8. Stritof.

9. Lopez, p. 191.

10. "George Lopez," *Newsmakers*, Issue 4, Gale Group, 2003, <http://galeschools.com/hispanic_heritage/bio/lopez_g. htm? (December 8, 2007).

11. Lopez, p. 80.

12. Ibid., pp. 84–85.

13. Ibid., p. 86.

14. "Gift of Life From a Comedian's Wife."

15. Ibid.

16. Interview with Larry King, "Interview with Ann and George Lopez."

17. Stritof, "George and Ann Lopez."

CHAPTER 5. ENTER SANDRA BULLOCK

1. George Lopez, *Why You Crying?: My Long, Hard Look at Life, Love, and Laughter* (New York: Touchstone Books, 2004), p. 102.

2. Ibid., p. 87.

3. Maria Elena Fernandez, "They're linked in spirit and schedule: George Lopez and Freddie Prinze Jr. have a special connection, and so do their TV shows," *Los Angeles Times*, October 17, 2005, E1.

4. Lopez, p. 101.

5. "Biography," *George Lopez Online*, 2002, <http://www.georgelopez.com/bio/bioinfo.html> (November 8, 2007).

6. Roger Ebert, "Bread and Roses," *Chicago Sun Times*, June 1, 2001. <http://rogerebert.suntimes.com/apps/pbcs.dll/article?AID=/20010601/REVIEWS/106010301/1023> (December 8, 2007).

7. Steve Simels, "Bread and Roses: Review," *TV Guide*, n.d., <http://online.tvguide.com/newsearch/detail.aspx?tvobjectid=135200&more=ucmoviereview> (November 12, 2007).

8. Lopez, p. 98.

9. Roger Ebert, "Real Women Have Curves," *Chicago Sun Times*, October 25, 2002. <http://rogerebert.suntimes.com/apps/pbcs.dll/article?AID=/20021025/REVIEWS/21025 0310/1023> (December 8, 2007).

10. "George Lopez," *Newsmakers*, Issue 4, Gale Group, 2003. <http://galeschools.com/hispanic_heritage/bio/lopez_g.htm> (December 8, 2007).
11. Ibid.
12. Lopez, pp. 101–103.
13. Ibid., p. 112.
14. Phillip Rodriguez, "Brown is the New Green: George Lopez and the American Dream," *PBS*, August 18, 2007.
15. "George Lopez," Newsmakers, Issue 4, Gale Group, 2003, <http://galeschools.com/hispanic_heritage/bio/lopez_g.htm> (December 8, 2007).
16. Lopez, p. 117.
17. Hector Saldaña, "Review: Comic Lopez, Free of Censors, Cuts Loose and Hilarity Ensues," *San Antonio Express-News*, July 2, 2006, p. 4B.
18. Lopez, p. 126.
19. Ibid., pp. 126–127.
20. Ibid., p. 118.
21. Ibid., pp. 115,119.
22. Ibid., p. 116.
23. Ibid., p. 123.
24. Ibid., p. 125.
25. Ibid., p. 127.
26. "George Lopez," *Newsmakers*, Issue 4, Gale Group, 2003, <http://galeschools.com/hispanic_heritage/bio/lopez_g.htm> (December 8, 2007).

CHAPTER 6. THE GEORGE LOPEZ SHOW

1. Bruce Lee Smith, "Comedian Laughing from School to Sitcom," *George Lopez Online*, December 21, 2001, <http://www.George Lopez.com/news/01_07.html> (November 12, 2007).

2. "Behind the Scenes: Production Meeting," *Ifilm*, May 27, 2007, <http://www.ifilm.com/search?query=2836953&s=Search> (November 5, 2007).

3. George Lopez, *Why You Crying?: My Long, Hard Look at Life, Love, and Laughter* (New York: Touchstone Books, 2004), p. 129.

4. Ibid., pp. 113–114.

5. Ibid., p. 114.

6. Ibid., p. 46.

7. "George Lopez: The Show," *George Lopez Online*, 2002, <http://www.George Lopez.com/theshow/theshow.html> (November 12, 2007).

8. "Dyslexia Information Page," *National Institute of Neurological Disorders and Stroke*, February 13, 2007, <http://www.ninds.nih.gov/disorders/dyslexia/dyslexia.htm> (November 12, 2007).

9. Amanda Shank, "Lopez Sitcom to Deal With Teens, Steroids," *USA Today*, May 8, 2005, <http://www.usatoday.com/sports/preps/2005-05-08-lopez-steroids_x.htm> (November 12, 2007).

10. Ibid.

11. "George Lopez Season 1 Episode Guide," *Yahoo! TV*, 2007, <http://tv.yahoo.com/George Lopez-lopez/show/30654/season/7043;_ylt=AtWALX3xQC_qzdxwY6qyRrFvV4V4> (November 12, 2007).

12. "50 Greatest TV Dads of All Time," *TV Guide*, June 20, 2004, <http://www.tv.com/georgelopez/person/64037/biography.html> (December 11, 2007).

13. Lopez, p. 104.

14. Phillip Rodriguez, "Brown is the New Green: George Lopez and the American Dream." *PBS*, Sptember 12, 2007.

15. Ibid.

16. "Biography," *George Lopez Online*, 2002, <http://www. georgelopez.com/bio/bioinfo.html> (November 8, 2007).

17. "Ford's Theatre National Historical Site," *National Parks Service*, June 26, 2005, <http://www.nps.gov/archive/ foth/index2.htm> (November 12, 2007).

18. Lopez, p. 6.

19. Ibid., p. 7.

20. Ibid., p. 7.

21. Ibid., pp. 5–8.

22. Ruben Navarrette, "Being George Lopez," *The San Diego Union-Tribune*, February 18, 2007, p. G3.

23. "George Lopez's Grammy Coup," *TV Guide*, September 3, 2003, <http://www.tvguide.com/News-Views/ Interviews-Features/Article/default.aspx?posting= {FBFE2DE7-1493-4B78-8853-858B4729EA94}> (November 12, 2007).

24. Navarrette, p. G3.

Chapter 7. "America's Mexican"

1. George Lopez, *Why You Crying?: My Long, Hard Look at Life, Love, and Laughter* (New York: Touchstone Books, 2004), p. 11.

2. Hector Saldaña, "Review: Comic Lopez, Free of Censors, Cuts Loose and Hilarity Ensues," *San Antonio Express-News*, July 2, 2006, p. 4B.

3. Ruben Navarrette, "Being George Lopez," *The San Diego Union-Tribune*, February 18, 2007.

4. George Lopez, "America's Mexican," *HBO Special*, February 24, 2007.

5. Lopez, *Why You Crying?*, p. 2.

6. "George Lopez," *Internet Movie Data Base*, 2007, <http:// www.imdb.com/name/nm0520064/bio> (November 12, 2007).

7. James Poniewozik, "George Lopez, the Prime-Time Funny Man," *Time*, 2005, <http://www.time.com/time/nation/article/0,8599,1093636,00.html> (December 9, 2007).

8. Lopez, *Why You Crying?*, p. 48.

9. Marilyn Beck and Stacy Jenel Smith, "George Lopez Promises Immigration Jokes on HBO's 'America's Mexican,'" *National Ledger*, February 23, 2007, <http://www.national ledger.com/cgi-bin/artman/exec/view.cgi?archive=9&num=11764> (December 9, 2007).

10. Phillip Rodriguez, "Brown is the New Green: George Lopez and the American Dream," *PBS*, August 18, 2007.

11. Interview by Larry King, "Interview with Ann and George Lopez," *CNN.com*, June 9, 2005, <http://edition.cnn.com/TRANSCRIPTS/0506/09/lkl.01.html> (Nov. 2, 2007).

12. Maria Judnick, "Forever Lions: Jessica Hanson," *Los Angeles Loyolan*, August 2007, <http://media.www.laloyolan.com/media/storage/paper803/news/2005/08/30/Sports/Forever.Lions.Jessica.Hanson-971997.shtml> (November 7, 2007).

13. *Jenna Johnson Obituary*, n.d., <www.jennajohnson.org> (November 5, 2007).

14. Ramona Shelburne, "Their gift is a running tribute," *Daily News*, March 18, 2006, <http://www.highbeam.com/doc/1G1-143596984.html> (November 12, 2007).

15. Hilary Howard, "Q&A George Lopez," *NCGA Golf Magazine*, Summer 2005, pp. 18–21.

16. Email from Ed Vyeda (Caddyshack Award), Hunter Public Relations, Special Events, Pebble Beach, California (November 7, 2007).

17. "The 25 Most Influential Hispanics in America," *Time*, August 22, 2005, p. 1.

18. Dave, Lake, "Q & A With George Lopez: 'America's Mexican' Sits Down for a Quick Chat About His Upcoming

HBO special," n.d., <http://tv.msn.com/tv/article.aspx?news=252453> (November 11, 2007).

19. Lopez, *Why You Crying?*, p. 3.

20. "George Lopez," *VideoETA*, 2007, <http://videoeta.com/person/1434> (November 12, 2007).

21. Lopez, *Why You Crying?*, p. 135.

22. Ibid., p. 136.

23. Ibid., p. 142.

24. Ibid., pp. 142–143.

25. Ibid., p. 139.

26. George Lopez, *El más chingón*, (Regando Beach, Calif.: Oglio Records), 2006, Track #1.

27. George Lopez, *Right Now, Right Now*. 2002.

28. Lopez, *El más chingón*.

29. Jamie Malanowski, "How Funny People Got that Way," *Readers Digest*, September 2004, <http://www.rd.com/content/famous-comedians-paths-to-stardom/2/> (November 12, 2007).

30. Lopez, *Right Now Right Now*.

31. Lopez, *Why You Crying?*, p. 91.

32. Lopez, *Right Now Right Now*.

33. Lopez, *Why You Crying?*, p. 156.

34. Ibid., p. 139

35. "Naughty or Nice," *The Wonderful World of Disney*, n.d., <http://abc.go.com/movies/naughtyornice.html> (November 9, 2007).

36. "The Adventures of Shark Boy and Lava Girl in 3-D Synopsis," MovieFone, 2007, <http://movies.aol.com/movie/the-adventures-of-shark-boy-and-lava-girl-in-3-d/19470/synopsis> (November 5, 2007).

37. Joe Leydon, "The Adventures of Sharkboy and Lavagirl in 3-D," *Variety*, June 3, 2005, <http://www.variety.com/review/VE1117927299.html?categoryId=31&cs=1> (December 11, 2007).

38. Robert Ebert, "The Adventures of Shark Boy and Lava Girl in 3-D," *Chicago Sun Times*, June 9, 2005. <http://rogerebert.suntimes.com/apps/pbcs.dll/article?AID=/20050609/REVIEWS/50605001/1023> (December 8, 2007).

39. "George Lopez," *Internet Movie Data Base*, 2007, <http://www.imdb.com/name/nm0520064/bio> (November 12, 2007).

40. "For Fourth Consecutive Year, Oprah is America's Top Favorite TV Personality," *The Harris Poll® #12*, February 3, 2006, <http://www.harrisinteractive.com/harris_poll/index.asp?PID=636> (November 12, 2007).

41. "The 25 Most Influential Hispanics in America," *Time Magazine*, August 22, 2005, <http://www.georgelopez.com/news/05_04.html> (November 12, 2007).

42. "George Testi-Lies for Benny," ABC Primetime Programming Guide, *George Lopez Show*, Season 6, Episode 4, Air Date: February 14, 2007, <http://abc.go.com/primetime/George Lopez/en/episodes/2007/4.html> (November 12, 2007)

43. *George Lopez Online*, 2005, <http://www.George Lopez.com> (November 12, 2007).

Chapter Eight. A Hole-in-One for George

1. "The PGA Tournament," *The Golf Channel*, January 17, 2007.

2. "Visionary Award," TV Land Awards, 2007, <http://www.tv land.com/video/index.jhtml?bcpid=192889081&bclid=2022 17748&bctid=196439147> (November 9, 2007).

3. George Lopez, *Why You Crying?: My Long, Hard Look at Life, Love, and Laughter* (New York: Touchstone Books, 2004), p. 47.

4. Maria Elena Fernandez, "They're Linked in Spirit and Schedule: George Lopez and Freddie Prinze Jr. Have a Special Connection, and So Do Their TV Shows," *Los Angeles Times*, 2005, p. E1.

5. 2004, TV Land Visionary Award, Recipient—*Chico and the Man*, *TV Land Video Clips of Classic Television and Original Series*, March 7, 2004, <http://www.tvland.com/video/index.jhtml?bcpid=192889081> (November 12, 2007).

6. "George Lopez," *Internet Movie Data Base*, 2007, <http://www.imdb.com/name/nm0520064/bio> (November 12, 2007).

7. Hollywood Walk of Fame Recent Ceremonies Hollywood Chamber of Commerce, 2007, <http://www.hollywoodchamber.net/icons/recent_ceremonies.asp#George Lopez> (November 12, 2007).

8. Fernandez, p. E1.

9. Ibid.

10. Ibid.

11. "Hollywood Walk of Fame Recent Ceremonies," *Hollywood Chamber of Commerce*, 2007, <http://www.hollywoodchamber.net/icons/recent_ceremonies.asp#George Lopez> (November 12, 2007).

12. Fernandez, p. E1.

13. Gerry Gittelson, "Comedian Lopez Proves He's a Survivor," *Daily News*, November 12, 2001, <http://www.georgelopez.com/news/01_06.html> (November 12, 2007).

14. *PGA.com*, 2007, <http://www.pga.com/home/pgaofamerica/> (November 11, 2007).

15. "George Lopez to host PGA TOUR special 'Every Moment Counts' Dec. 24 on ABC," *PGATour.com*, December 13, 2006, <http://www.pgatour.com/info/company/story/9868998/> (November 9, 2007).

16. "Bob Hope Chrysler Classic: The Eagle has Landed," *PGA Tour.com*, 2007, http://www.pgatour.com/tournaments/r002/> (November 12, 2007).

17. Jill Painter, "Lopez Filling Starring Role: Comedian Brings the Celebs Back," *Inland Valley Daily Bulletin*, January 17, 2007, <http://www.dailybulletin.com/search/ci_5028025> (November 12, 2007).

18. Ken Peters, "George Lopez picks up the golf mantle for Bob Hope," *Associated Press*, January 17, 2007, <http://www.nctimes.com/articles/2007/01/18/sports/professional/23_01_211_17_07.txt> (November 12, 2007),

19. Ibid.

20. Paul Oberjuerge, "Lopez Trying to Bring Hope Back to Classic," *Daily Bulletin*, January 17, 2007, <www.dailybulletin.com.ci-5028435> (March 2008).

21. Mark C. Anderson, "The Clown Prince of Golf. George Lopez Shows Pebble Beach How to Have Fun," *Monterey County Weekly*, February 8, 2007, <http://www.montereycountyweekly.com/issues/Issue.02-08-2007/cover/Article.cover_story_1/print> (November 12, 2007).

22. Oberjuerge.

23. Richard Ruelas, "Lopez Uses Fairway to Up Latino Image," *Arizona Republic*, February 2, 2007.

24. Hilary Howard, "Q & A George Lopez," *NCGA Golf Magazine*, Summer 2005, pp. 18–21.

25. Lopez, p. 16.

26. Ibid., p. 116.

27. Painter.

28. Ruelas.

29. Peters.

30. Jeff Shelley, "Barrow Discusses First Tee Program,"
    Cybergolf, 2007, <http://www.cybergolf.com/jeffs
    Journal/index.asp?newsID=2364> (November 12, 2007).

31. Lopez, p. 182.

32. *Starlight Starbright Children's Foundation*, n.d., <www.
    starlight.org> (November 7, 2007).

33. "Love, Hope, Respect," *We Care for Youth.org*, 2002,
    <http://www.wecareforyouth.org> (November 12, 2007).

34. Ruben Navarrette, "Being George Lopez," *The San Diego
    Union-Tribune*, February 18, 2007, p. G3.

35. Oberjuerge.

36. "Comedian To Help Fight Kidney Disease Since Having A
    Kidney Transplant, "*National Kidney Foundation of Southern
    California*, October 4, 2005, <www.kidneysocal.org/New
    _Folder2/George Lopezannpr.doc> (November 11, 2007).

37. Bella Mahaya Carter, "George and Ann Lopez share the gift
    of life," *Studio City Sun*, Vol. 4, No. 7. March 24–30, 2006,
    <http://suncomm.globat.com/~suncommu/
    archives/studio_city_sun_archives/2006/March%2024/
    STU_032406.pdf> (November 11, 2007).

38. Sheri and Bob Stritof, "George Lopez and Ann Serano [sic],"
    About.com: Marriage, 2007, <http://marriage.about.com/
    od/quotes/a/George Lopezann.htm> (November 12,
    2007).

39. Interview by Larry King, "Interview with Ann and George
    Lopez," *CNN.com*, June 9, 2005, <http://edition.cnn.
    com/TRANSCRIPTS/0506/09/lkl.01.html> (Nov. 2, 2007).

40. *George Lopez Online*, 2005, <http://www.George
    Lopez.com/home/home.html> (November 12, 2007).

41. "Obesity," *Healthline*, 2007, <http://www.healthline. com/adamcontent/obesity?utm_term=obesity&utm_ medium=mw&utm_campaign=article> (November 12, 2007).

42. "Actors Julia Louis-Dreyfus and George Lopez Host New Video to Fight Childhood Obesity Epidemic," *eMedia Wire*, 2005, <http://www.emediawire.com/releases/ 2006/6/emw404988.htm> (November 7, 2007).

43. "George López recibe un transplante de riñón," *People en Español*, February 2007, <http://www.people enespanol.com/pespanol/articles/0,22490,1054529,00. html> (November 12, 2007).

44. "Lopez Five Things," *American Library Association*, 2006, <http://www.ala.org/lopez> (November 10, 2007).

CHAPTER 9. WHAT'S NEXT?

1. George Lopez, *Why You Crying?: My Long, Hard Look at Life, Love, and Laughter* (New York: Touchstone Books, 2004), p. 16.

2. "Getting Punked," *Punk'd*, Season 5, first aired Sunday July 3, 2005, <http://vids.myspace.com/index.cfm?fuseaction= vids.individual&videoID=1295753754> (November 12, 2007).

3. Lopez, p. 161.

4. *George Lopez Online*, 2005, <http://www.George Lopez.com/home/home.html> (November 12, 2007).

5. "Balls of Fury," *Internet Movie Data Base*, 2007, <http:// www.imdb.com/title/tt0424823/> (November 12, 2007).

6. Dave Lake, "Q & A with George Lopez: 'America's Mexican' Sits Down for a Quick Chat About his Upcoming HBO Special," n.d., <http://tv.msn.com/tv/article.aspx?news =252453> (November 11, 2007).

7. "Star Spanglish Banter," *HBO Special*, February 24, 2007, <http://www.hbo.com/events/georgelopez_07/index.html?ntrack_para1=leftnav_category3> (November 12, 2007).

8. Marilyn Beck and Stacy Jenel Smith, "George Lopez Promises Immigration Jokes on HBO's 'America's Mexican,'" *National Ledger*, February 23, 2007.<http://www.national ledger.com/cgi-bin/artman/exec/view.cgi?archive=9&num=11764> (December 9, 2007).

9. "George López recibe un transplante de riñón," *People en Español*, February 2007, <http://www.peopleenespanol.com/pespanol/articles/0,22490,1054529,00.html> (November 12, 2007).

10. Lake.

11. Paul Oberjuerge, "Lopez Trying to Bring Hope Back to Classic," *Daily Bulletin*, January 17, 2007, p. 117.

12. "100 Most Influential Hispanics," *People en Español*," January 4, 2007. <http://www.hispanicprwire.com/news.php?1=in&id=7796&cha=7> (December 11, 2007).

13. Maria Elena Fernandez, "ABC pulls plug on 'George Lopez,'" *Los Angeles Times*, May 16, 2007, p. E1.

14. "Television Syndication," *Museum of Broadcast Communications*, 2006, <http://www.museum.tv/archives/etv/S/htmlS/syndication/syndication.htm> (November 12, 2007).

15. Phillip Rodriguez, "Brown is the New Green: George Lopez and the American Dream," *PBS*, August 18, 2007.

16. Ruben Navarrette, "Being George Lopez," *The San Diego Union-Tribune*, February 18, 2007, G3.

17. Lake, "Q & A with George Lopez: 'America's Mexican' sits down for a quick chat about his upcoming HBO special."

18. Ted Fass, "Entertainers: George Lopez," *Entertainment Unlimited*, 2007, <http://www.tedfass.com/entertainers/c5/details812-1/George Lopez-Lopez.html> (November 12, 2007).

19. Gerry Gittelson, "Comedian Lopez proves he's a survivor," *Daily News*, November 12, 2001, <http://www.george lopez.com/news/01_06.html> (November 12, 2007).

20. "November 2007 Calendar," *The Ice House*, 2007, <http://www.icehousecomedy.com/cgi-bin/calendar/long_calendar.cgi> (November 2, 2007).

21. Hector Saldaña, "Review: Comic Lopez, free of censors, cuts loose and hilarity ensues," *San Antonio Express-News*, July 2, 2006, p. 4B.

22. Navarrette.

23. Ibid.

24. Scott Gummer, "Looping for Lopez," *Golf Magazine*, n.d., <http://www.georgelopez.com/news/05_02.html> (November 11, 2007).

25. Lopez, p. 87.

26. "Sixty Seconds Life Story: George Lopez," *TV Guide Channel*, n.d., <http://online.tvguide.com/celebrities/George Lopez-lopez/151657> (November 11, 2007).

Glossary

anesthesia—A drug that makes a person unconscious for an operation.

Anglo—An English-speaking person who is not of Hispanic descent.

arthoscopic surgery—Surgery where a small incision is made and pencil sized instruments are used to look inside the patient's body during the procedure.

Chicano—Mexican American.

circuit board—The place where microchips and other computer parts are located.

dementia—A gradual loss of memory; people with dementia often do not know their names or where they are.

dyslexia—A learning disability; someone with dyslexia has trouble with spelling and reading but is of normal intelligence.

epilepsy—A physical condition caused when nerve cells in the brain misfire; sometimes caused by an injury to the brain.

Latino/Latina—A person who was born, or is descended from a person who was born in a Spanish-speaking country in the Western hemisphere.

memento—Souvenir; something that reminds.

migrant—A worker who moves from place to place looking for work.

producer—A person who supervises or pays for a television show or a movie.

revolution—The overthrow of a government, usually by violence.

seizure—A sudden attack brought on by a disease; shaking uncontrollably, losing consciousness.

Spanglish—A mixture of Spanish and English.

stereotype—A general opinion or a judgment of a group.

supplement—A product taken by mouth that adds vitamins, minerals, and other substances to the diet.

therapy—Treatment, especially of a bodily, mental, or behavioral disorder.

tradition—Customs that are passed down from generation to generation.

3-D—Three dimensional; a type of film that gives the impression of depth.

Spanish Vocabulary

¡ay!—oh!

barrio—A Spanish-speaking neighborhood.

buenos días—Hello (good morning).

calzones—Underwear; shorts.

chorizo—Pork sausage highly seasoned with chili powder and garlic.

churros—A pastry made by deep-frying dough and sprinkling it with sugar.

estaban—Were.

güeros—Light-skinned people.

loco—Crazy.

mira—Look.

sabes que—You know.

tía—Aunt.

tortilla—A piece of round, flat bread.

vato—Slang for "dude."

zapatos—Shoes.

Further Reading

BOOKS

Brooks, Tim and Earle Marsh. *The Complete Directory to Prime Time Network and Cable TV Shows (1946–Present)*. New York: Ballantine Books, 1999.

Guzmán, Lila and Rick Guzmán. *George Lopez: Comedian and Television Star*. Berkeley Heights, N.J.: Enslow, 2006.

Hill, Anne E. *Sandra Bullock*. San Diego, Calif.: Lucent Books, 2001.

Jordan, Victoria. *Freddie Prinze, Jr.: A Biography*. New York: Pocket Books, 2000.

Lopez, George. *Why You Crying: My Long, Hard Look at Life, Love, and Laughter*. New York: Touchstone Books, 2004.

INTERNET ADDRESSES

George Lopez
<www.georgelopez.com>

George Lopez television show
<www2.warnerbros.com/georgelopez/index.html>

National Kidney Foundation

Index